INFORELIEF

Stay Afloat
in the InfoFlood

Maureen Malanchuk

Jossey-Bass Publishers • San Francisco

This publication is designed to provide accurate and authoritative information in regard to the subject matter covered. It is sold with the understanding that the publisher is not engaged in rendering legal, accounting, or other professional service. If legal advice or other expert assistance is required, the services of a competent professional person should be sought. From a Declaration of Principles jointly adopted by a Committee of the American Bar Association and a Committee of Publishers.

Compositor: Lee Ann Hubbard
Cover Design: Paul Bond
Cover Illustration: Kathleen Blavatt
Editor: JoAnn Padgett
Interior Design: Lee Ann Hubbard
Production Editor: Dawn Kilgore

Published by Jossey-Bass
United States of America

Editorial Offices: 415-433-1740
Orders: 800-956-7739

Printed in the United States of America

Printing 1 2 3 4 5 6 7 8 9 10

ISBN: 0-7879-0347-7

Library of Congress Cataloging-in-Publication Data

Malanchuk, Maureen.
    INFORelief : stay afloat in the InfoFlood / Maureen Malanchuk.
        p.   cm. — (Warren Bennis executive briefing series)
    Includes bibliographical references and index.
    ISBN 0-7879-0347-7 (hard)
    1. Personal information management. 2. Information resources management. 3. Information technology—Management. 4. Time management. I. Title. II. Series.
    HD30.2.M354 1996   96-18619
    658.4'038—dc20   CIP

Dedication

To Randy, for his love and support.

To Marlene, for helping me find the courage and the creativity.

Contents

Editor's Preface

Information overload—what Maureen Malanchuk refers to as the "infoflood"—is one of the most pervasive and potentially debilitating challenges of modern working life. In our home lives we've learned ways to tune out most of the extraneous messages and clutter that compete for our attention. In our working lives, knowing as we do that information is power, we try to absorb everything—and as a result often drown in the process.

In the search to filter, use, and make sense of the infoflood, people look to their leaders to bring direction, understanding, and coherence to their work: it is one of the most basic expectations followers have of leaders. Part of the job of the leader—of any effective performer—is to make mere data into meaningful information and to elevate information to useful knowledge. Yet the greater your level of responsibility the greater the volume, complexity, and consequence of the information you confront—and the greater your obligation to effectively communicate with others.

That is what makes Maureen Malanchuk's work so important. In clear, concrete terms she addresses a problem that confronts all of us. For most organizations, information is a basic resource. And understanding how to manage that resource can give busy executives a decisive edge in their own careers and in their ability to lead others. Maureen's advice ranges from the practical (to reduce the flow of info clutter, skip anything you would not pay for) to the strategic (develop a dedicated channel of communication for moments of organizational crisis).

As Malanchuk also makes clear, the connection between personal success and organizational success is never so evident as in the handling of information. How you handle voice mail, e-mail, journals, memos, and reports says a lot about your management style and skill.

And as electronic media become more a part of life, your information-handling skills may also determine your access to information and influence with others. Likewise, how companies collect, organize, and distribute information says a great deal about their strategies, values, and responsiveness. Increasingly, information about your core service or product can have as much value as the core product itself—but only if you know how to use it.

Information overload is not going to abate. The sea of information we all must negotiate in work life is only going to rise. Maureen Malanchuk offers us a lifeline: grab it!

Warren Bennis
Santa Monica, California

Author's Preface

I wrote this book to get back at all those people who, over the years, flooded me with information. I also wrote it to atone for my contribution to the glut.

Before

Sales manager Jacob Smithers runs into his office early Monday morning after trying to relax at his cottage during a four-day vacation. Calls from the office disturbed him only 8 times—a record.

As he sits down at his desk, the phone rings and a colleague tells him that he will drop off the department's reengineering plan before lunch so Jacob can familiarize himself with it before tomorrow's meeting. After warning Jacob that the plan is 267 pages long, the colleague hangs up.

Jacob swivels in his chair to log onto his electronic mail system and finds 207 new messages waiting for him.

At that moment, another colleague walks into his office and asks Jacob if he saw the baseball game on Sunday. After complaining for ten minutes about the sloppy playing of a highly paid outfielder, the colleague leaves.

Out of the corner of his eye Jacob sees a foot-high pile of paper. When he turns his head, he sees his mail from the last few days: the pile contains 76 letters and memos (most of which are 3-4 pages long), 15 brochures from suppliers, 22 magazines and trade publications, and 8 newsletters. He transfers the pile to his three-foot high "to read" pile.

He spots 6 sales reports sitting next to this paper pile; a handwritten note on top informs Jacob that the people who sent them are expecting responses before the end of the day today. Before he can reach for the first report, his phone rings and the national sales director on the other end tells him to attend an important meeting at 10:00 a.m. this morning. As Jacob jots the meeting time and location on a little piece of paper that he promptly misplaces, the group's secretary walks into his office and welcomes him back from his vacation. She then hands him 67 pages of faxes and informs him that he's scheduled to attend 4 meetings today.

As Jacob contemplates this flood of information, he thinks of at least 3 current business books that he intended to read during his holiday, but didn't.

Overwhelmed by the piles of paper and electronic messages, Jacob reaches for the bottle in the top drawer of his desk. He swallows a couple of aspirin for the headache that has begun pounding like a jackhammer at the front of his skull.

Spotting the flashing light on his telephone, he picks up the receiver and punches in his access code. An electronic voice informs him that he has 65 new messages and 10 archived messages. It also informs him that his voice mail system is full and that it has not been accepting new messages for the last 24 hours. Jacob hangs up the phone, hesitates for a moment, then picks it up again and dials his home number. When his wife answers, he asks her to cancel their tickets for tonight's theater performance, telling her he will be working late. With his tongue only slightly in his cheek, he tells her that if he is lucky he might make it home again by Friday.

Jacob replaces the receiver and swivels his chair back to his computer screen. With a sigh, he hunts and pecks with two fingers and brings the first electronic message onto the screen. It is a new accounting policy. Not sure what to do with it, Jacob closes it and leaves it on his system. He brings up the next electronic message, a retirement notice...

Overview

The first step in managing a flood is to determine whether you are in the middle of one.

This chapter

♦ Identifies symptoms so that you can assess whether you are suffering from information overload.

♦ Outlines a general strategy for dealing with the flood, as well as the benefits of doing so.

ARE YOU DROWNING?

Anyone who isn't confused here doesn't really understand what's going on.

Nigel Wrench, English journalist and commentator

1

WHAT IS INFORMATION OVERLOAD?

A flood is "any great outpouring or stream: a flood of tears." When something floods, it overflows, deluges, overwhelms. So it is with information.

Information overload is what happens when you are drowning in a flood of information. It occurs when you are overwhelmed by too much information, too quickly, too often, and have not yet developed the skills to manage the torrent. You are particularly susceptible to information overload in your professional life or in your job. Your livelihood and continued success depend on how well you manage information (among other things) whereas the implications of missing an episode of your favorite sitcom or the latest issue of a general-interest magazine are considerably less serious. Information

1

overload is caused by an information flood that shows no sign of slowing down or stopping.

There are a number of symptoms of information overload. Do you

❏ Feel unable to keep up with everything?

❏ Resent information-related duties because they steal time from your "real" job?

❏ Work with the constant fear that you are missing important information?

❏ Suffer from "information paralysis"? (The inability to proceed from the question or problem to beginning to gather information for the answer or solution because there are too many sources and you don't know where to start?)

❏ Suffer from "analysis paralysis"? (The inability to make a decision or act on something because you are receiving too much information—much of it contradictory.)

❏ Complain that you get too much irrelevant information and never enough important or relevant information?

❏ Suffer from lapses of memory?

❏ Feel guilty about that growing stack of periodicals waiting to be read?

❏ Hear from colleagues and business associates that they cannot get through to you because your voice mail is either always turned on or always full?

WAISGLASS/COULTHART

"Greg never got around to reading all of his memos on Friday."

❑ Feel as if you will burst from all the propaganda you receive and the corporate-speak you are forced to mouth?

❑ Take information home every night or feel like you should to keep up?

❑ Feel chained to the office 24 hours a day now that you have a cellular phone and laptop computer?

WHAT'S THE SOLUTION?

Managing an information flood can be done in seven steps. These seven steps are outlined in this book.

The Steps to Manage an Information Flood

1. Are you drowning?

2. What causes information overload?

3. Stay calm.

4. Assess your situation.

5. Develop information-receiving skills.

6. Reduce your contribution.

7. Don't fall in again.

Though it is difficult to develop new skills when flailing about in the middle of a flood, finding yourself in such a situation also provides plenty of incentive.

WHY BOTHER?

Learning to manage an information flood will

♦ Boost your confidence in your ability to handle information tasks effectively

♦ Help you complete information tasks better and faster, thereby increasing your efficiency and productivity

♦ Reduce time spent trying to find or understand information

♦ Help reduce your confusion and stress levels at work

♦ Reduce your frustration with, and maybe even increase your enjoyment of, all those nifty electronic gadgets sitting on your desk

♦ Free you from simply trying to cope with the information flood so that you can use information strategically for competitive advantage

♦ Help you discern what information really matters, thereby minimizing your susceptibility to publicity, propaganda, or manipulation

♦ Better prepare you to handle problems and crises when they occur

♦ Help you feel safer and more secure in an increasingly complex, chaotic world

♦ Give you more time to spend with loved ones

Organizations that learn how to float in the information flood will

♦ Suffer fewer lost business opportunities since information will be clearer and fewer messages will be lost

♦ Improve corporate memory about important policies, procedures, and programs by learning how to produce and store them most effectively

♦ Improve communications with both customers and suppliers

♦ Produce both internal and external communications that reflect your desired image of an effective, competitive organization

♦ Reduce employees' paper burden so they can easily access and identify current, important information, which will facilitate better, more timely decisions for your organization

♦ Enjoy lower communication costs by eliminating duplication and waste, streamlining processes, and improving targeting (One estimate puts the business cost of government red tape in the United States alone at $166 billion annually.[1])

♦ Enjoy higher productivity and employee morale and a reduced learning curve

The Three Mile Island Information Disasters*[2]

An example of poor information management was the accident at the Three Mile Island nuclear reactor in 1979. Though serious engineering, technical, and management failures contributed to the disaster, so did poor information management. For example, early information about the potential for an accident had been ignored.

Two and a half years before the event, two senior Babcock and Wilcox engineers sent a formal memorandum to management expressing concern about faulty equipment that could cause a "meltdown." The warning was submitted on the wrong form, misdirected, and ignored.

The engineers persisted, asking at least that operators at Three Mile Island be instructed not to interfere with the emergency pumps if they ever kicked on. The customer service department agreed to add those instructions to the operating guidelines, but nothing was done and the message never got out.

During the same time, Aerospace Corporation reported to the Nuclear Regulatory Commission that the control room at Three Mile Island was very poorly engineered from a human factors standpoint and that it would be a severe handicap if ever a crisis were to occur. The report was stamped "for future resolution" and forgotten.

In May 1978, the shift supervisor at Three Mile Island sent a strongly worded memo to his superiors saying the feedwater system that regulated the pressure inside the reactor was subject to failure that might cause "very significant" damage. He suggested remedies and urged immediate action, but his memo was ignored.

UPI/Bettmann News Photos

*In 1979 a nuclear power plant located in Three Mile Island, Pennsylvania, underwent a partial meltdown. Although very little radiation leaked into the atmosphere, the results were panic among nearby residents, the loss of billions of dollars, and severe criticism of nuclear power programs.

SUMMARY

Information overload is what happens when you are overwhelmed by too much information too quickly too often and have not yet developed the skills to manage the torrent.

Symptoms of information overload include feelings of anxiety, fear and frustration directed at the information you receive, those sending it to you, and your inability to handle it effectively.

Learning to manage an information flood benefits both you and the organization for which you work by reducing confusion, helping you focus on priorities, and increasing your productivity.

OVERVIEW

Five factors contribute to the huge quantity of information flooding your life:

♦ Technology

♦ The nature of information

♦ Social trends

♦ Business trends

♦ Corporate information cultures

Understanding the various causes will help you determine which solutions will best help you manage your information flood.

What Causes Information Overload?

2

The Causes

Technology adds to the flood by allowing us to produce and distribute huge volumes of information quickly and easily, and increases the pressure on us to process it just as quickly. The nature of language and the limited "shelf life" of information make it challenging to communicate messages clearly in a timely manner.

Social and business trends place great value on information and a corresponding pressure on us to produce it. Corporate information cultures perpetuate ineffective communication practices that damage the credibility and quality of most organizational information.

A decade ago it might have taken a week to write, produce, and distribute a memo. Today we are asked to produce that memo in a matter of hours or minutes. And we are asked to do this several times a day.

TECHNOLOGY

Information technology, such as computers and faxes, contribute to information overload by allowing us to produce a phenomenal quantity of information quickly and easily, and to distribute it to numerous locations almost instantaneously. Consider the following:

♦ As information technology capabilities increase or expand, so do the expectations of, and demands on those using them. A decade ago it might have taken a week to write, produce, and distribute a memo. Today we are asked to produce a memo in a matter of hours or minutes. And we are asked to do this several times a day.

60 billion faxes were sent in 1991 from U.S. fax machines.[1]

♦ Growing numbers of workers have access to computers, e-mail, and faxes. As it becomes easier and quicker for more people to contribute to the information flood, technology has eroded time and geographic boundaries, making it increasingly difficult to shut off the flood or ignore it. It does not take long for conveniences such as "call forwarding" and modems that allow you to access your office phone and e-mail messages from home to change from being a perk to being a pest. Many of us have experienced the "convenience" of receiving nightly e-mails from our bosses, or the "freedom" of working all weekend from home.

Some 25 million e-mail nodes are linked. Experts predict the number of users will grow by 20% to 30% per year, while the number of messages per user will increase 25% annually.[2]

♦ In spite of more and better information channels, they are still far from perfect with many bugs— technological and otherwise—to work out, such as software that freezes when you input a certain command, people using different versions of a software program, or uneven access across an organization. While you are expected to do more, faster, you also must contend with technological glitches that undermine efficiency and increase stress levels.

♦ Most companies focus on providing employees with hardware and software while placing less emphasis on complementary communication skills. We are entering the Information Age with phenomenal new tools and are still using Industrial Age communication skills, treating information as if it were a product on an assembly line. We have not yet learned how to ensure that all the information we add to the flood is meaningful and effective, or how to become better all-around communicators.

♦ In addition, we do not receive enough technological training to use software to help us filter the infoflood that arrives on our desk every day or to use our communication channels such as e-mail, voice mail, and regular mail as an information system rather than as half a dozen disconnected communication islands.

Schools often emphasize memorization, recognition, and regurgitation of data rather than analysis and understanding. Not only are many of these skills outdated, but most of us did not do a very good job developing the foundation of effective communication: reading, writing, and speaking. We are discovering that our wondrous technology does not automatically make us better communicators.

Management guru Peter Drucker estimates that the transition to the new society (which he calls the "Knowledge Society") will not be completed until 2010 or 2020.[3]

WAISGLASS/COULTHART

"Still haven't figured out how to send e-mail, huh, Bob?"

Using All the
Buttons

**75% or more of
electronic products'
features and
capabilities are not
used.**[4]

♦ Technology may be faster, but that does not mean our work is better. Most current business processes (including communications) were designed in the 1950s, before the arrival of modern information technology. Most of these processes have not changed much since then. For example, at the same time that we can communicate virtually anywhere in the world almost instantaneously, we often must run material through a number of hierarchical approvals or distribution channels.

♦ Finally, technology adds to the flood by creating stress that hampers our abilities. Computers and information technology are a major source of stress. When we become stressed, higher-level thinking processes such as memory, logical reasoning, idea production, and decision-making suffer. The nervous activation of the brain combined with the increased flow of stress hormones causes whole portions of the brain to more or less shut down their activities. Complex mental tasks present much more difficulty when we experience the tension of a pressure-filled situation than when we are fully relaxed. So while technology provides more information faster, it also impairs our ability to process that information efficiently.

THE NATURE OF INFORMATION

Roughly 1.6
trillion pieces of
paper circulate
through American
offices annually.[5]

The nature of information adds to the flood in a number of ways. For example, information tasks (analyzing data, solving problems, thinking critically or creatively) are difficult to evaluate, so information is often viewed as a means of accomplishing something or producing something else rather than an achievement on its own. Most performance review systems still are based on the industrial system that rated people according to the number of widgets produced, the time required to produce those widgets, or the percentage of those widgets that met certain standards. What gets measured gets done well; what does not get measured either does not get done or gets done poorly. We seldom measure the effectiveness of information or communication, so standards are low and quality poor.

Other characteristics inherent in the nature of information affect both the quantity and quality of material we receive. Consider the following:

More information has been produced in the last 30 years than in the previous 5,000.[6]

♦ It is very easy for messages to be confusing or misinterpreted.

The more information is repeated, the more likely it will change or be incorrect as each person adds their own interpretation, bias, and twist. Inconsistent or contradictory messages result.

The total of all printed knowledge doubles every 8 years.[7]

♦ It is much easier to "dump" information than it is to communicate it effectively.

Unless you have the same skill with words that Mozart had with music, the communication process usually requires some thinking, crafting, editing, and rewriting.

The writing process, for anything other than a simple e-mail message, requires time and concentration. In today's fast-paced business world, we are usually short on both.

♦ Information's dynamic nature means it becomes dated quickly and must be updated regularly.

♦ The value of information is subjective and may change depending on the situation or timing. A message that means nothing when delivered can have a completely different meaning in a couple of days, or even in a couple of hours. This can make us indecisive about what to do with the information.

Your judgment about information may also change depending on whether you are writing or reading it. How many of us send out 20-page reports full of facts and figures but prefer to get a one-page analysis or summary?

♦ The speed at which information multiplies also adds to the flood. For example, a single scientific finding may result in four magazine articles, two television documentaries, a multimedia exhibit for a local science center, and the pursuit of six new areas of research.

♦ Information channels, such as newsletters and magazines, have an insatiable appetite for content even when there is no news or important information to report. There are companies and services whose entire business is to provide packages of ready-to-use articles, columns, and other "filler material," complete with illustrations and designs. Customers can even get this information on disk. We are bombarded with extraneous information and are left to separate the significant from the insignificant.

♦ As information becomes an increasingly powerful currency, people and organizations are creating new ways to exploit it and use it to contribute to their bottom line. There are many new forms of information, and we do not always know how to differentiate or prioritize them. Examples of this are the special magazines produced by companies to promote their products and services to customers.

Information is data that has been processed and given relevance and purpose.

It helps when you are processing information to be aware of both the type of information you need and the form of information that you receive. Data and information are external experiences. Data can be measurements, observations, or facts. It can flow one way and is often measured by bits or volume. It can be transmitted without a human receiver or sender. Information is data that has been processed and given relevance and purpose.

> *"Where is the wisdom we have lost in knowledge? Where is the knowledge we have lost in information?"*
> —"The Rock," T.S. Elliot

Knowledge, understanding, and wisdom are internal experiences. Knowledge is the facts or experiences known by a person or group of people—known being consciousness or familiarity. Understanding is the ability to learn, judge, or make decisions. It is also your interpretation of a subject. Wisdom is the ability to think or act by using knowledge, experience, understanding, common sense, and insight.

Instructions and education are forms of information intended to help you do or learn something. Marketing, advertising, publicity, and promotional information are used to boost sales or the organization's image, or to influence public opinion. New hybrid forms of information, such as edutainment and infotainment, combine entertainment with education (interactive software) or information (extended advertisements on TV).

SOCIETAL FACTORS

A number of societal factors also contribute to the information flood. In an agricultural society, we used face-to-face communication and intuition or experience to know when, where, and how to plant crops or raise cows. In an industrial society, we needed technical and procedures manuals to tell us how to do things in the plant or on the assembly line. In an information society, we manage and manipulate information for a living. We don't grow or make things any more—we talk about things. We "grow" or "produce" information.

Today's pace of life increases stress levels and reduces efficiency, making us less successful in managing information. Many people suffer from chronic overload or the "acceleration syndrome"[8] —the feeling of constantly being behind schedule. Symptoms include:

❑ Rushing your speech

❑ Completing other people's sentences

❑ Eating rapidly

❑ Becoming impatient at waiting in line

❑ Feeling like you can never catch up

❑ Scheduling too many activities for time available

❑ Detesting "wasting time"

❑ Driving too fast

❑ Trying to do several things at once

❑ Becoming impatient if others are too slow

❑ Lacking sufficient time for relaxation, intimacy, or the enjoyment of your environment.

Other societal factors contribute to information overload by affecting the world in which we live and the role that information plays in that world.

♦ The larger government's role is in society, the more information is required to fulfill that role.

♦ In today's increasingly complex society, we need more consultants and specialists to help us collect and analyze complex information.

♦ Increasingly, we are global citizens even if we never travel outside our own country. The eroding value of the dollar abroad, a new product launch in Japan, or a coup in Korea all can impact our life; therefore, we want or need to know about them.

♦ Now that you have your own families and also may be taking care of aging, ailing parents, you have other demands on your time and less time to devote to information duties than did the workaholic "yuppies" of the late 1980s.

♦ You are less willing to give up personal time to get caught up on reading and other information tasks and resent it when you are expected to do so. Overwhelmed and overloaded, you seek balance in life and recognize the value of home and hearth. You want to "downshift" from 14-hour days and "cocoon" at home, but the flood of information makes this almost impossible. This conflict increases frustration levels.

BUSINESS TRENDS

The direction, quantity, and force of information in most organizations has changed and this can also contribute to your overload problem. In the Industrial Age, information was top-down printed material, such as memos. Employees received information about operations, such as how to run a particular machine. In the Information Age, the torrent of information is fast and furious: it comes at us from all directions, through many communication channels, on a wide variety of topics.

A number of other business trends contribute to the infoflood by producing and requiring more information.

♦ Of the 75 percent of the work force employed in the service industry, 55 percent are employed specifically in information services.[9]

Most of these people spend their time researching, preparing, storing, revising, analyzing, and

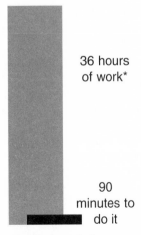

Workload vs. Time to Do It[10]

36 hours of work*

90 minutes to do it

*Stacked on desk on an average day

In Canada the electronics industry is larger than the pulp and paper industry; communications and telecommunications is larger than petroleum and mining combined. In the U.S. more people make computers than cars.[11]

communicating information, from the professor seeking be published to the PR person sending out a news release to the consultant on a speaking tour promoting his or her latest book. Even those not specifically employed in information services conduct a variety of information tasks.

♦ Many of us are also working longer hours. Working 14- to 16-hour days and weekends produces more information and adds to the flood.

Typical Daily Tasks Performed By Employees[12]

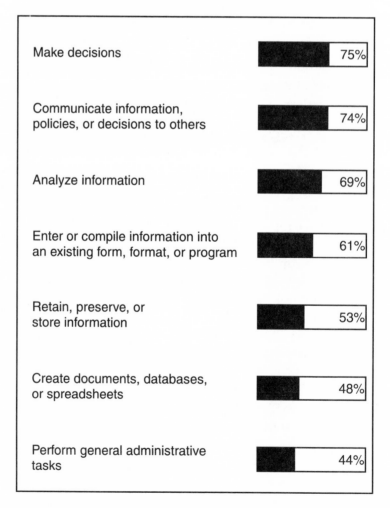

Task	Percentage
Make decisions	75%
Communicate information, policies, or decisions to others	74%
Analyze information	69%
Enter or compile information into an existing form, format, or program	61%
Retain, preserve, or store information	53%
Create documents, databases, or spreadsheets	48%
Perform general administrative tasks	44%

◆ Business has become a stormy sea of change. Managers have less control and more people. At the same time, "restructuring," "right sizing," and "downsizing" force us to do more with less.

CORPORATE INFORMATION CULTURES

[A] member of any organization is, in large measure, the kind of communicator that the organization compels him to be.

W. Charles Redding, communications specialist

Information cultures in most organizations promote communication practices that undermine the credibility and weaken the quality of messages—flooding channels with meaningless, confusing information. Some of these communication practices are intentional, others have become an ingrained part of the corporate culture.

◆ Peter Drucker says that there are whole layers of managers whose major role is to serve as "relays" or human boosters to pass on the faint, unfocused signals that pass for communication within traditional pre-information organizations. As the people in these managerial layers are increasingly laid off, the signals become fainter and more unfocused.[13]

Info-Tactics

Guided leaks = Leaks strategically targeted to powerful or influential forces, such as the media.
Masked source = True source hidden behind a more credible, less contentious one.
Double-channel ploy = Different messages communicated through different channels.
Access tactics = Controlling access to a powerful person, such as a CEO or a boss and, hence, the information they receive.
Need-not-to-know = When knowing something would necessitate action or imply agreement or compliance.
Forced-to-know = Also known as Cover Your Ass; sharing information to share responsibility or blame.

In the book *Horse Sense*, which outlines how you can develop a personal marketing strategy, the authors compare corporate politics to a horse race. They describe several horse races you can choose from and give you the odds of winning each race. Publicity has 10 to 1 odds and is the best course for someone who doesn't have a product (5-1 odds), person (3-1), or spouse (2-1) to tie their star to. Publicity or self-promotion does, however, beat out creativity (25-1 odds), company loyalty (50-1), and hard work (100-1).[15]

♦ Since information is power, there is often a strong desire to hoard it or to use it to your advantage. Reasons to manipulate information include saving face, covering your ass, making your boss look good, self-preservation, and self-promotion. Alvin Toffler outlines a number of "info-tactics,"[14] or ways to manipulate the delivery of information including guided leaks, masked source, double-channel ploy, and—on the receiving end—access tactics, need-not-to-know, and forced-to-know. Though all of his examples are from the political arena where knowledge has always been power, these tactics are playing an increasingly important role in corporate life by confusing messages and adding to the flood.

♦ In many organizations, the political agenda supersedes the informational one. This makes messages "muddy." Do we want colleagues to understand a new process or do we want to please the boss? Do we want employees to know what is going on in our department or do we want to receive a promotion? The answers to these questions will determine the success of our communications.

♦ Being human, your ego (or your boss's) can also result in decisions about information that are not in the best interest of your audience. Communications is often the most creative and fun aspect of a project. It confers power and prestige on the person doing the "talking," whether through a bulletin, report, or half-hour video. People, especially executives with large egos, like to see their pictures or names in print.

♦ Keeping employees in the dark about what the company is doing or where it is going contributes to the information flood because without a sense of direction, it is hard to prioritize information.

We end up reacting to all of the information we receive, unable to differentiate "urgent" from "important" or "nice to know" from "need to know" because we have nothing to measure it against.

♦ Differences exist between what senior managers want to say and when they want to say it and what employees want to know and when they want to know it. Organizational messages are often general and corporate-wide rather than outlining local implications, such as what does the new corporate policy on quality mean to the data entry clerk in the accounting department or the technician in the field?

♦ There are few linkages between messages and little context; each message is treated as a separate island. We are inundated with unrelated, confusing, even contradictory bits of information instead of meaningful explanations or context.

♦ Organizations increasingly recognize the importance of communications but continue to obfuscate the messages. This adds to the information burden because employees neither understand nor believe what is being said and must read between the lines to decipher the real message. One example of this softcore propaganda is the use of neutered, meaningless words or euphemisms such as "downsizing" for layoffs, "budget reductions" not "cuts," and "strategize" instead of "plan."

The Council for Communication Management found that 61 percent of all employees do not believe management tells them the truth.[17] Corporate communicators agree. Almost three-quarters of the more than 200 employee communications managers polled by consultant William M. Mercer say they tell employees only part of the truth.[18]

The Information Gap[16]

FORTUNE 500 Executives

82% believe corporate strategy is understood by everyone who needs to know

Employees

Less than 30% say management provides clear goals and direction

Another example of softcore propaganda is when an organization does not "walk the talk"; when the implicit messages are different from the official line. A huge gulf between the official line and what is seen or experienced undermines an organization's credibility. Common examples include the following:

What They Say vs. What They Do

Employees are our most important resource	When we have to cut costs, employees are the first to go
We value team players	We promote individuals
We like people to tell it like it is	Just tell us the good news; we shoot messengers of bad news
Customers are our number one priority	Exceed your sales quota and you get a bonus

♦ Quality, or lack thereof, also adds to the weight of your information burden because so many of the messages we receive are incomprehensible or confusing.

This lack of quality could be caused by intentional obfuscation and political agendas, but a lot of it is caused by weak communication skills, such as reading and writing.

♦ Information is often produced and distributed for its own sake. People want to communicate, but do not have anything of value or of interest to say. During my career, I have written many memos and speeches for which I did not receive

What's That You Say?

95% of the 2,000 letters, memos, and reports randomly drawn from one company's file had to be read more than once to be understood.[19]

any direction from the people who would be presenting them. The speakers had nothing to say but wanted to talk. Another time, a client asked me to prepare a promotional brochure about a speaker before she received details on what the speaker would be speaking about.

◆ The role of communications in most organizations also adds to the flood because it is treated as a last-minute "nice to do" instead of a key strategic tool. When communicating, there is often little planning done to determine "why," they are saying something, which would then clarify what should be communicated and how.

Information is often the quick-fix answer to more complex, long-term processes and solutions. One example of this is the fads that are given lip service but never really implemented. Business trends, such as employee empowerment, continuous improvement, and total customer satisfaction, often become little more than "flavor-of-the-month" fads. Examples of this are quality programs that consist of posters, task forces, and a newsletter and little else, or change programs centered around bulletins and executive travelling road shows.

Information also often is used as a catch-all; the easy way to recognize employees achievements, committee work, corporate announcements, position changes, retirements, weddings, obituaries, and other "nice to know" information from around the organization.

◆ There is a lack of attention and action dedicated to the problem. Everyone complains about information overload but few people do anything about it.

A poll taken at an International Association of Business Communicator's annual conference

Since 1959, consumption of writing and printing paper has gone from less than 7 million tons to more than 24 million tons per year.[20]

found that the top five issues in internal communications identified were as follows:[21]

1. Building management support

2. Promoting or communicating quality

3. Providing faster, more timely information

4. Building trust/credibility with employees

5. Managing a multicultural work force

"Dealing with media clutter" was ranked fourth for issues in external communications. Also, most communications departments are more concerned with formal communications or communications products, such as memos, than with informal communications processes such as e-mail or voice mail.

BIOLOGY

The final factor contributing to information overload is that many of us appear to have been born without the "contributor chromosome" that would allow us to recognize that we contribute to the information flood. Computers do not write memos and reports; voice mail does not leave messages; we do.

SUMMARY

The sheer quantity of information being produced today is one of the major causes of information overload; however, there are a number of other contributing factors.

Technology provides us with the speed and distribution systems that make it so easy for so many people to send so much information to so many so quickly. The nature of language and news makes it challenging to communicate clear, concise messages in a timely manner. Social trends, such as cocooning and the "sandwich generation," shift our focus away from workaholic habits. At the same time, business trends, such as empowerment and downsizing, increase our workload and make information an increasingly valuable commodity.

The outdated, ineffective communication cultures that exist in most organizations add to the information flood by using soft-core propaganda and obfuscation.

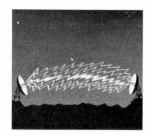

Overview

Once you have determined that you are suffering from information overload and have a better understanding of the causes, the next step is to remain calm. Thrashing about during a flood only makes things worse as you struggle to keep your head above water. Fight the urge to panic so you can assess the situation properly and then determine the best course of action.

This chapter will help you

♦ Develop a new perspective toward information and an appreciation of its role and value in the Information Age

♦ Recognize the opportunities inherent in an information flood

STAY CALM

Everyone spoke of an information overload, but what there was in fact was a non-information overload.

Richard Saul-Wurman, *What-If, Could-Be*

3

GAIN A NEW PERSPECTIVE

It is frustrating to be flooded with information. The natural reaction is either panic or paralysis. Unfortunately, neither approach gets projects completed and off your desk.

Remind yourself throughout the day—and throughout your life—that all those messages and memos are, after all, only information. Most of them are neither life nor death, nor—in the larger scheme of things—do most of them matter all that much. The trick is to identify and focus on those messages that are critical and to let the rest flow by. There are many things you can do to reduce and redirect the flood of paper and electronic messages and you will read about them in later chapters.

Also remember that communication is at the heart of all information technology. It does you and your organization little good if you are a computer whiz who can manipulate data in infinite configurations but you cannot convince your colleagues to contribute to a new project, your boss to purchase new widgets, or your company to improve a product or service.

SET REALISTIC GOALS

It is not realistic to expect that you will be able to stop the flood, but you can manage it and change your feelings and perceptions toward it. Realize that you will never catch up; that you will never be able to totally control your information flow—there will always be more filling in behind it. Revise your goals and try not to fall too far behind. Realize that you are not going to be tested on all the details of the information that comes across your desk. Remind yourself that you do not have to memorize everything. Instead, settle for knowing how and where to access the information when you need to. Be proud of accomplishing that much. Acknowledge and celebrate the information tasks you do accomplish instead of always focusing on what still needs to be done.

Determine the level of knowledge and expertise you want to develop and then work to develop it. Do you want total control? To be well-informed? To know what is important? To be aware of crises? To just know enough to get by? Unless you are a perfectionist workaholic, acknowledge that you cannot deal with a flood of information the same way you deal with a trickle.

Immediate memory is limited to about seven "chunks" of information. Most people can remember about seven numbers in a row, seven colors, seven shapes, or seven of any other item. So if you need to remember more than seven items, it's better to organize them into a smaller number of chunks.[1]

Another good piece of advice is to work smarter, not harder. When you are overwhelmed and drowning at work, a common response is to tense up and work even harder in an attempt to catch up and maintain control. You do the same things, only more of them. That means arriving earlier and staying later, seeing more people with problems, doing more paperwork, laying more pressure on, and pressing your nose even more tightly against that old grindstone.

Stress levels rise, emotional exhaustion begins, your personal life suffers, cynicism taints awareness, and, before you know it, coping mechanisms such as caffeine, drugs, or alcohol creep in.[2] Use the guidelines in this book to help you focus on your priorities and to set limits so this does not happen to you.

Stop Idolizing Information

Information and information technology are both just tools. Drop outdated values about information that you developed back in primary school, such as revering books and magazines and hesitating to mark them up or tear out pages. Tear out articles you want to read and recycle the rest of the magazine.

Also, with the proliferation of desktop publishing that allows anyone to produce and distribute information quickly and easily, don't assume that just because it is in writing or on a communication channel that it is true, accurate, or significant information.

Suspend Self-pity

This is not the first time in history that people have had to develop new attitudes toward information and learn new communication skills, and it won't be the last.

While you're purging yourself of self-pity, you may as well ditch the wishful thinking too; the problem won't go away. With the pace of technological innovation, it will only get worse . . .until you start making it better.

DON'T FEEL GUILTY FOR DEALING WITH THE PROBLEM

Ignore that nagging little voice in your head telling you that you have more important things to do than manage information. You don't. If your information is out of control, so is the rest of your job. Making time to manage information is just as important as visiting clients or meeting project team members.

APPLY CONVERSE LOGIC

When things get particularly tough, such as the day an eight-inch pile of reports lands on your desk for discussion at the afternoon meeting, consider what it would be like to suffer from information underload. What would it be like not to have enough information? Imagine . . .

♦ Being unaware of a dangerous situation near your home or office, such as a gas leak or a train derailment

♦ Misjudging a product launch because you had not read the market research report

♦ Being unaware of a client's or competitor's bankruptcy

♦ Being unaware of a potential supplier's previous embezzlement conviction

♦ Being ignorant about areas of political unrest or cultural sensitivities when planning a business trip to that area

♦ Not knowing about sales or bargains and paying double the price

♦ Being unaware of effective new business trends that your major competitor is already using

♦ Feeling boring and uncomfortable at business receptions or cocktail parties because you have nothing to talk about

♦ Making professional gaffes and hopping around the office with your foot in your mouth because you're not aware of who's doing what to whom when.

Suddenly information underload doesn't sound quite so appealing anymore. A more effective alternative would be to try to get your information overload problem under control.

A busy front-line supervisor with 64 staff members once complained that he received too much information, and then proudly informed me that he handled it by not paying attention to any of it. "If it's really important, someone will come and tell me," he said. Though information overload can be a problem if not managed correctly, his approach is like ignoring the knock in your car until the transmission falls out. While it is true that the really important information will eventually catch your attention, by that time it likely will have exploded into crisis proportions. That means you could learn about it by reading the front page of your local newspaper or when a customer serves you with legal papers. It also means that you will miss lots of valuable information that is not critical enough to make it to your office door.

LOOK ON THE BRIGHT SIDE

Information overload is not just an irritating problem; it is also a great opportunity. In order to take advantage of the new source of power in the Information Age, you must learn to manage the information that floods your desk or computer screen and recognize how to use that information to your best advantage. Some of that information could help you identify client needs, suggest new services or products, or make a stronger business case for your project proposal.

GIVE YOURSELF SOME ELECTRONIC SPACE

. . . even if that means turning your communication channels off. It can also mean simply not continually logging into your e-mail or responding to the flashing light on your voice mail.

Learn to give yourself some "electronic space" just as you have come to expect a certain amount of personal space. Without this electronic space, you can feel constantly overwhelmed by information.

RELAX

Take a deep breath. And another one. Gaze out a window for a few minutes, if you have one nearby.

It is hard to read a report or respond to a memo when you are in the flight or fight response—hands shaking, and breathing fast and shallow.

HAVE SOME FUN WITH INFORMATION

If you see managing your information flood as a chore, then it will become one. Since you are going to be spending some time on information tasks regularly, you may as well try to make them something you enjoy doing. Play around a bit. Be willing to experiment with solutions to the flood. If something doesn't work for you, try something else. Use the advice in this book as a guide. Ask friends and colleagues how they deal with information overload and try some of their solutions.

STRIVE FOR BALANCE

When working with information technology, balance the rush for quantity with an appreciation for quality. Balance broadness with depth.

Balance speed of keystrokes with minutes of reflection. One good decision, creative idea, or simple solution is more of an accomplishment than shuffling two inches of paper or twenty e-mail messages.

Balance life with computer work and play. Get away from technology. Get a life. Gardening, cooking,

Anybody Home?

A principal scientist for Toronto's Alias Research, Inc., a manufacturer of high-end computer graphics software, such as that used in the movie *Jurassic Park*, has linked his door to a mouse, which is linked to the videophone in his computer. When his door is closed, the videophone does not ring. He has also linked his computer to a camera mounted on his office wall. Those trying to reach him on the Internet get a picture: a closed door means do not disturb him, leave a message; an open door showing him at his desk means that you can reach him.[5]

WAISGLASS/COULTHART

"We're trying to reduce the paperwork."

hiking, tai-chi, yoga; do anything that gets you closer to nature or yourself and away from machines—particularly information machines.

BE PREPARED TO COMMIT THE TIME AND EFFORT

I'll be honest with you (cause you're going to find out eventually anyway): managing an information flood is neither quick nor easy. It won't happen overnight. Getting your problem under control goes a lot faster, however, when you commit the time and energy up front to accurately define your particular problem, and then streamline and organize your flood. This approach is also a lot more effective than flailing and fighting every day from 7:00 a.m. to 10:00 p.m. trying to keep your head above water.

TAKE THE NEXT STEP

Now that you have shifted your perception to see the opportunities inherent in an information flood, it is time to find out more about your particular problem(s) with information. Do you receive too much information? Or just too much of the wrong stuff? Do you get too much from several sources, or does most of the flood originate from one or two people?

SUMMARY

In order to survive and thrive in an information flood, you must stay calm and gain a new
appreciation for information.

Information is simply a tool you can use
to make decisions or take action. It will not
provide all the answers to your questions, nor
will it solve all your problems. In an Information Society, however, it is becoming an
increasingly powerful currency. By learning
what information is important to you and your
company, you can learn to use information to
your advantage while ignoring information
that merely distracts you from your purpose.

You can gain this new perspective toward
information by setting realistic information
goals, giving yourself some electronic space,
and learning how to let the flood flow.

OVERVIEW

The next step toward inforelief is to assess your particular information flood and to identify your preferences and weaknesses in dealing with it.

To deal with an impending flood, experts study the environment and collect data about the potential flood, such as the barometric pressure at the eye of a hurricane or rainfall data—information that helps forecast flood conditions. This information helps determine what steps should be taken to manage the flood or to minimize damage.

Similarly, in an information flood, you must study your flood of information and identify trends. Observing your information flood and getting to know its character and quirks is a critical step in identifying the best solutions for dealing with it.

ASSESS YOUR SITUATION

Many managers find themselves reading [all] this stuff coming into their box in order to determine whether they ought to be reading it at all.

Frank Nunlist, Assistant Postmaster General

4

DON'T SKIP THIS STEP

Although it is tempting to skip this chapter and rush straight to the part that offers solutions, fight the urge to do so. Before rushing in with solutions, it is a good idea to take some time to define your problem. Readers who skip this short section may end up fixing the wrong problem.

Vague, unfocused complaints about the large volume of information you receive do not have any impact on the problem and sap energy better directed toward solving the problem. The more you know about your particular information flood, the better your chance of successfully managing it.

The following assessment is a simple but powerful tool to help you identify what your problem is, not just what you think it is. You may be amazed at what this exercise helps you discover about your information flood and your ability to handle it.

Not only is analyzing your results enlightening and useful, but so is the process of collecting the data. It helps you become more conscious or aware of information habits that have become automatic, but which are not necessarily effective.

USE SHORTCUTS

There are technological shortcuts that can help you assess your information flood quickly and easily:

- ◆ Most e-mail systems allow you to click on an icon to regroup incoming messages according to sender, date, or topic; outgoing messages can be grouped according to recipient, date, or topic.

- ◆ If you will be recording a lot of data, use a spreadsheet program to help you keep track of your flood and automatically add up numbers, or use the "find" function on your word processing program to locate key words in documents.

CREATE AN INFORMATION PROFILE

How to Create an Information Profile

1. Complete this exercise before you read the rest of the book.

2. Do not change information habits or do what you think you are supposed to be doing. Simply observe and record.

3. Identify an average two-week period to monitor and chart your information flood. Try to capture a normal period of time, rather than a particularly heavy or light one.

4. If you cannot dedicate a two-week period to this task, chart your information flood for at least one week. A day is better than nothing, but it will not be as useful to identify trends.

5. Create a simple chart and fill it out daily. (There is a blank "Incoming Information" chart in the Appendix that you can photocopy and enlarge.) Answer the questions below about each piece of information that you receive at work or related to work, whether written, verbal, or visual.

   Unless you have more than two to three long, personal conversations a day at work, do not track them.

6. If your schedule is really hectic and you do not even have the extra five or ten seconds to fill out the chart, consider having your secretary or executive assistant shadow you and record the flood for you.

7. Study your data to identify trends Also identify your strengths and weaknesses in dealing with the information. Do you have a good memory and comprehend ideas quickly? Are you well-organized and decisive? What is your personality type (intellectual or intuitive, action-oriented or a dreamer)? What are your communication preferences; do you prefer to see routine information in writing or to handle it with a quick phone call?

   When completing the chart, use codes to save time, effort, and space. Examples follow:

Where	Channel
Desk - D	E-mail - EM
Hallway - H	Voice mail - VM
	Fax - F
	Mailbox - MB
	Telephone - T
	Face to Face - F2F

Sample Information Profile

Incoming Information

when	who	where	channel	topic	purpose	my response	why	reaction
8:00 a.m.	Janet	H	F2F	course	discuss	discuss	career	interest
8:00	Suzanne	H	F2F	meeting	inform	agreed to attend	my project	distaste
9:30	Jim	D	EM	project "A"	update	trash	no interest	frustrated
10:15	Pat	D	EM	budget cuts	request for info	respond & delete	project leader	weary and peeved
10:15	prof. assoc.	D	MB	trade journal	inform	skim & file	career info	some interest
10:15	CEO	D	MB	Mission Statement	inform	trash	propaganda	cynical
10:15	Human Res.	D	MB	new procedure	?????	trash	confusing	confused
10:15	???	D	MB	stress	survey	trash	no interest	peeved
10:15	Wade	D	MB	reorg.	FYI	put in "to read" file	too long	neutral
10:20	Suzanne	H	F2F	work	assignment	respond	job	neutral
10:30	Paul	D	F	newsletter	estimate	file	job	neutral
11:45	Pat	D	T	product launch	request for info	agreed to send	my project	weary and peeved
12:00 p.m.	Jim	D	EM	project "B"	update	trash	no interest	irate
2:00	Janet	D	VM	CEO letter to the editor	requested copy	agreed to get copy	crisis	fear, anxiety
2:00	Mary	D	VM	newsletter	respond to my call	replied on VM	job	neutral
2:00	Lucy	D	VM	budget cuts	FYI	noted and delete	project leader	neutral
2:00	CEO	D	MB	Mission Statement	inform	trash	propaganda	cynical
2:30	Barb	D	T	CEO letter	respond to my call	info. noted	crisis	more anxiety
2:30	Ann	D	VM	CEO letter	respond to my call	respond and delete	crisis	relief

Note Preliminary Trends

Following are some initial problems or trends from my sample Information Profile. If they continue over a significant period of time, I should take steps to reduce or eliminate them.

♦ I received two copies of the CEO's memo about the Mission Statement—my manager sent me a second copy even though the original was addressed "to all employees." Also, it was too "Rah Rah" and abstract for me. (10:15 and 2)

♦ The memo from the Human Resources Department was gobbledygook and I had no idea what they were trying to tell me. (10:15)

♦ Pat requested copies of two documents that I had already sent her; either we have a distribution problem or she has a filing problem. (10:15 and 11:45)

♦ I have no idea who sent the survey about stress or how the results will be used. Therefore, I threw it out. (10:15)

♦ Jim always sends project updates that have nothing to do with me and that I'm not interested in. (9:30 and 12)

♦ The document from Wade was too long for a status report (75 pages). Also, it did not include a summary and repeated a lot of information from previous reports. (10:15)

Information Profile Trend Analysis Questions

Answer the following questions when completing your Information Profile.

When

When (in approximate terms) do you receive the information? Did a single piece of information straggle in on its own, or did a whole pile appear at once? In most offices, some information arrives at a regularly scheduled time each day, such as mail delivery at 10:00 a.m. and 2:00 p.m. and the bulletin boards or news flashes first thing every morning after they've downloaded the messages into everyone's computer system. Other things, like phone calls, voice mail, faxes, and e-mail can and usually do arrive continuously throughout the day.

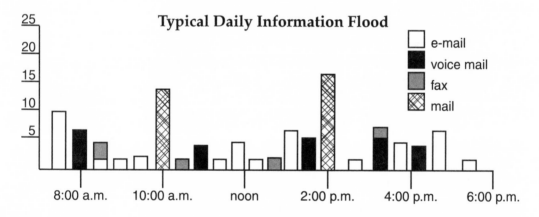

Other trends can be monthly or seasonal. Information floods are often a little slower in July and August when a lot of people take vacations. There is often another breather between Christmas and New Years. The really busy times might be just before year-end when everyone is trying to spend their budget, or during major sales campaigns.

Who?

Who sends the information? Is it coming from your boss, human resources, or accounting? Is it coming from your colleagues? Peers? Subordinates? Is it coming from all those people and from everyone else too?

Following are some culprits guilty of common communications crimes that tend to clog up communications channels. Do you recognize any of them? Do any of them sound like you?

What?

What channel or media is the information coming in on?

E-mail, bulletin boards, reports, memos, brochures, phone calls, fax, voice mail? The trade magazines you should be reading every month to keep up-to-date on what's happening in your profession? All those electrifying presentations, productive meetings, and conference calls that you participate in every day? Together with the copious reports to take back and study in greater detail? The half dozen newsletters received every week from various groups and organizations? And then there are videos. And what about the countless conversations you have every day?

"We must be on a mailing list."

FARCUS © FARCUS CARTOONS. Dist. by UNIVERSAL PRESS SYNDICATE.
Reprinted with permission. All rights reserved.

Common Communication Culprits and Their Crimes

Alias	Identifying Information Habits
Boomerang Boss	Forwards all information to you whether that information has anything to do with you or not. Never indicates why it was sent to you or what you are expected to do with it.
Bureaucratic Babbler	A trivia nut, this conscientious bore sends out retirement notices, new appointments, and new procedures that are never of any interest to anyone else.

Common Communication Culprits and Their Crimes (continued)

Confused Clod	Sends confusing messages, unclear memos, and meaningless reports.
Distribution Demon	Sends everything to everyone, especially information that is of interest to no one.
Incontinent Imp	Goes on and on about the background and rationale of a project before finally getting to the point in the last sentence of a four-page memo.
Literal Lawyer	Writes everything out in formal complete sentences, never uses charts or graphs, and prefers pages and pages of numbers. Uses big words and long sentences. Often uses jargon.
Paranoid Prude	Sends follow-up memos on every conversation and informal meeting. Confirms every statement and decision in writing.
Publicity Pig	Sends daily status reports, all seven drafts of a report, minutes of meetings, and play-by-play commentary on every office activity to let the whole world know what he is doing or has done.

What is the content or topic of each message?

Is it about a project you're working on? A presentation someone's giving next week? A company baseball game tomorrow?

Why?

Why do you receive the information? Were you being asked a question? Were you asked for some information? Were you asked to do something? Are they trying to educate you about helpful business tips? Is it about a new trend like Total Quality or Employee Empowerment? Or merely to inform you? Are they trying to persuade you? Are they trying to sell you something? Are they trying to convince you to do something, i.e., vote for someone or take your vacation days before the end of the year?

Why did you respond the way you did? Do you need to stay plugged in to what's going on? To be on top of things at meetings? To understand what's happening in your business? To put out fires? To help you achieve career goals? To keep up with late-breaking business news?

Where?

Where do you receive the information? At your desk? In the elevator or hallway? At the water cooler? At lunch? On the golf course? In an airplane? At home late at night?

How?

How did you respond to the information? Answered a question? Provided more details? Passed the message onto someone else? Ignored it? Filed it? Acted on it? Read it and left it?

How do you feel about receiving it? Both the particular messages and the continual flood?

How much stress does it add to your life?

Were you curious and eager to read it? Or were you bored and resentful that someone was wasting your time?

Were you frustrated and irritated?

Fearful and anxious that you cannot keep on top of events and that you are going to miss something important one of these days? Embarrassed? Overwhelmed? Indecisive? Helpless? Happy? More confused?

Be careful here. This is probably the hardest part of this exercise. Identifying your feelings is hard and admitting to them is even harder . . . especially at work.

FOLLOW - UP WITH REGULAR CHECK - UPS

Do a mini or informal information assessment every couple of months to ensure that you are still dealing with the same flood. If it has changed direction or picked up speed it may require a new approach.

TAKE THE NEXT STEP

Develop the new information-receiving skills needed to survive in the Information Age and apply them to your particular situation as identified in your Information Profile. These skills are outlined in the next chapter.

SUMMARY

Familiarize yourself with the nuances of your particular information flood; your efforts to manage it will be more effective.

Creating an Information Profile makes it easier to identify trends in your flood, as well as your areas of strength and weakness in dealing with those trends. To create an Information Profile, observe and record your information flood over a two-week period, as well as your reaction to it. Identify the who, what, when, where, and why of all the information you receive.

OVERVIEW

Now that you have assessed your particular situation, it is time to learn how to stop drowning by managing your information flood. In learning how to swim, you were taught that if you are drowning you should conserve your energy, either by treading water or by drownproofing. You also were trained to call for help and to watch for opportunities or objects that could save your life.

In an information flood, you should also conserve your energy. This chapter will help you

♦ Develop survival skills that will help you quickly and effectively filter, find, and analyze a huge quantity of information in a chaotic environment.

♦ Become an assertive consumer of information instead of a passive victim.

DEVELOP INFORMATION - RECEIVING SKILLS

An individual without information cannot take responsibility; an individual who is given information cannot help but take responsibility.

Jan Carlzon, CEO, SAS

5

START AT THE BEGINNING

Before developing the information-receiving skills, think about your role, responsibilities, and goals. Write them out and review them every couple of months. Remain focused on these factors, but be flexible when new opportunities arise. Articulating these goals will help keep you focused and on target when coping with an information flood. It will also help you develop a sense of accomplishment in a flood that never ends.

♦ Goals and Objectives—Include both professional and personal and short- and long-term. Make these goals as concrete and specific as possible. For example, instead of saying I will find new clients, aim to increase your client base by at least 20 percent over the next year.

Familiarize yourself with your company's goals and balance them with the sometimes conflicting demands of customers' and suppliers' needs.

♦ Job Description—Write a new one that accurately reflects your information duties and incorporates your goals and objectives as well as your company's.

♦ Performance Appraisals—On performance reviews include information tasks and projects, such as major presentations, proposals or reports, and committees or meetings that you chaired. Remember to include the outcome of your efforts. Results could be anything from increased sales to a greater understanding of a new service to streamlining a reporting process or reducing message duplication.

DEVELOP INFORMATION-RECEIVING SKILLS

You may already be using some of the information-receiving skills to manage information; however, few of us have formally been taught how to use them most effectively.

1. SKIP

*"The more information one has to evaluate,
the less one knows."*

Marshall McLuhan

1. *Get rid of as much unnecessary and useless information as possible*—the paper pollution, the garbage, and the junk

Information-Receiving Skills

1. Skip   Reduce or eliminate the
                   unnecessary, useless
                   information you receive.

2. Screen   Monitor your information channels
                   and decide what to do with
                   incoming information.

3. Skim   Find and focus on the important
                   information in large documents,
                   reports, or books.

4. Scan   Quickly find specific information.

5. Search   Identify those information sources
                   that will be most valuable to you
                   and access them fast.

6. Surf   Sift the big picture from an ocean of
                   information.

7. Satisfice   Know when you have enough
                   information to make a decision or
                   communicate an idea.

mail. To determine what is the necessary or useful information, keep these elements in mind:

♦ Your purpose

♦ Revised job description

♦ Personal information profile from the previous chapter

♦ The type or purpose of the information—Is it to educate, inform, entertain, or persuade? Is it advertising, data, or educational material? Also take a look at the date, topic, and source or sender to help screen outdated or unimportant information.

♦ Importance and urgency of the information— also relevance to you and your goals and your level of interest.

> *Important information furthers your goals or your company's. Urgent information has to be dealt with immediately. Interesting information is "nice to know." Relevant information is "need to know."*

When deciding what information to skip, apply the 80/20 rule (also known as the Pareto analysis).

80 percent of useful information will come from 20 percent of our sources.

Identify that important 20 percent and focus attention and efforts there.

Determining what information you should skip can also help point out important information you should be receiving and are not.

2. *Avoid duplication.* Do you really need to read local, regional, *and* national newspapers? Do you really need to read a newspaper on the subway into work if you listen to the morning news on the radio? If the answer is yes, fine; if it is no, stop doing it.

3. *Contact people who regularly send information you have decided to skip and explain why their information is of little or no value to you.* If they can make it more valuable to you, reconsider your decision; if they cannot, ask them not to send it anymore.

4. *Plan a small window to accommodate political pressures and personal information preferences.* The key word here is "small." Include information you need to read because of who is sending it or because it is a politically important topic (but not necessarily an important corporate topic.) To do this, you will need to first identify your organization's important political players. Likewise, allow some information to filter through that is interesting but not necessarily relevant to your job. Don't get carried away.

What's It Worth to You?

Having trouble deciding what information to skip? Ask yourself what information you would be willing to pay for. If this still doesn't reduce the flood, ask yourself what information you'd be willing to pay for from your own wallet. This will quickly differentiate the "need to know" from the "nice to know."

2. SCREEN

"Some books are to be tasted, others to be swallowed, and a few to be chewed and digested."

Sir Francis Bacon

Screening is what you do when you regularly monitor your communication channels and decide what to do with each piece of information you receive.

1. *Develop an information monitoring or filtering system*—a method of regularly checking all of your major communication channels. Different channels require different monitoring. Voice mail and e-mail are inherently faster and require monitoring 2-3 times a day; mail can be screened once or twice a day. If you are expecting urgent, important information, you can either monitor your systems more often or, preferably, have someone hand-deliver the material to you. The best method of screening your information also depends on whether your flood is periodic or permanent.

Refer to the Information Profile you prepared in the previous chapter and determine when the major flux of information arrives in each of your channels, then schedule enough time to screen at common arrival times.

If your work schedule does not allow for such frequent screening, schedule some time—say first thing in the morning, after lunch, or before you leave for the day—to take another bite out of the beast.

Do not access your channels every time new information appears or that is what you will spend most of each day doing. If someone drops off urgent, important information and you are not dealing with something more urgent, deal with the new information at once.

2. *Dedicate some time—an hour, a day, a couple of days—to screen and unclog the information currently in your communication channels.*

3. *Spend no more than five to ten seconds screening each piece of information.* With practice, you will be able to reduce screening time to just a couple of seconds.

4. *Screen every piece of information and do something with it.* Move it further down your channels. Keep the information flowing. Do not simply return it to your information channel.

How to Screen Information

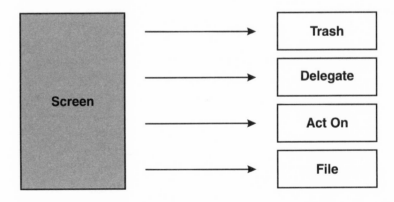

TRASH

♦ Immediately trash or recycle garbage, junk mail, and misdirected material.

Discard unnecessary information. This step is important because it allows you to concentrate on the information you keep. Holding onto garbage adds to your stress level and increases your guilt level.

♦ You might want to keep a special file as a safety net for the first couple of weeks to reduce anxiety about throwing material out. As you become a better screener, you will develop more confidence in your trashing decisions and eventually can remove this safety net.

DELEGATE

♦ Delegate information to someone else if they are better qualified to deal with it, or when you have more important priorities.

♦ Set-up some kind of exchange system with those whom you delegate to or exchange information with on a regular basis. Color-coded files or even a specific in-basket work well.

♦ Follow up after you forward or delegate information, or ask them to keep you up-to-date.

♦ Consider delegating some of your reading tasks. For this to work, you must give clear instructions about what you are looking for and how you want it presented, such as having key points highlighted or with an overview or summary.

ACT ON

- ◆ Act on as much information as possible as soon as you have screened it and determined that it needs to be acted on by you.

- ◆ If this approach does not work for you, set aside some time each day—at least half an hour—to take care of incoming, priority information that requires only a simple response, such as "yes," "no," or "talk to Joe." Schedule other more time-consuming information duties into whatever time-management system you use or add it to your "to do" list.

- ◆ If the action you need to do is read and you don't have time right then, rip out interesting articles or sections and file them for future reading, then discard the rest of the publication. (Do this only if there is no one else on the distribution list).

Learn to differentiate between various reading styles and to determine the most appropriate for each information task. The reading style you use depends on the complexity of the material and the degree of detail you need, your goals and current knowledge level, and the author's writing style. Readers may use more than one reading style when reading a single document, report, or book.[1]

- ◆ *Casual reading* is how you read general interest information, or "FYI" material. It is done at your normal reading speed.

- ◆ *Careful reading* will help you understand the information you are reading, such as that in a legal document. It is slower than your normal reading speed, and you may need to stop and think about something, or you may have to go back and read something over a second or even a third time.

♦ *Critical reading* will help you reach a decision after reading the information, such as okaying or vetoing a new project. For critical reading, you must be an active reader, taking notes, underlining or highlighting important sections, passing judgment on each point, asking questions and searching for answers. The slowest of all the reading styles, it is also the most active form.

FILE

♦ Decide which form will be your predominate filing system, paper-based or electronic, and stick to it. If you are filing electronically, purchase a scanner to scan information into your computer. If your filing system is paper-based, print out copies of important electronic documents and include them in the file.

♦ Important information that falls under the FYI category, or which is background information on a project, should be filed after it is read.

Facts About Files[2]

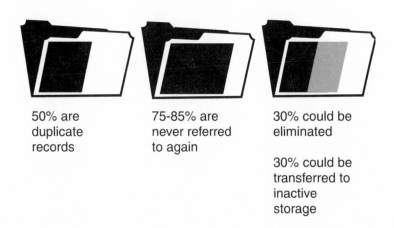

50% are
duplicate
records

75-85% are
never referred
to again

30% could be
eliminated

30% could be
transferred to
inactive
storage

♦ When filing information, keep the previous statistics in mind and have a trash bin nearby just in case that is a better option.

♦ Use a filing system that makes sense to you; one that is organized the way you naturally think. Papers can be filed either alphabetically (by name, subject, or location) or numerically (consecutive numbers, terminal digit, middle digit, chronological or deadline tickler).

♦ Develop some quick, easy method to get rid of obsolete files. Use a color-coded system to indicate permanent files, those that can eventually be stored, and those that can be tossed out. Some expert filers jot down the expiration date or month on each file, just like you find on a milk carton.

♦ Use sub-files within larger files for quick access to information.

♦ A Bring-Up File (BUF) ensures that information is acted on before the deadline. Some people use electronic systems, others jot the deadlines in their calendar or appointment book. Though a "pending" or "holding" file is better than nothing at all, it is not a preferred method, since you have to check it daily and go through a lot of information that you do not need to worry about yet.

♦ Use software to develop a set of automatic procedures or "rules" to delete, store, and categorize incoming e-mail. Some regular office productivity packages include such rules and filters.

After you have read e-mail messages, file those you want to keep. Don't forget to build in an option that allows you to save, delete, or archive old messages.

WHAT IFS

♦ If it is not possible to get rid of all the clutter in your system, make it your goal to move the clogs further down your system, away from your screening step, so that you are not constantly screening the same information.

♦ If you are lucky enough to have a "screener," such as a secretary or administrative assistant, some of the preliminary screening will be done for you, but you will still need to do some yourself. This person often looks after the follow-up function as well, reminding you of deadlines.

♦ If your company is large enough and the information load is heavy enough, train a "screener" for each department or division. This person would know generally that group's goals and priorities and could channel appropriate information through to them.

♦ Have someone else do some of the preliminary screening for you.

Subscribe to a local news clipping service. You determine the parameters, such as company name(s) or subject(s). If it is critical that you receive late-breaking news, subscribe to an electronic clipping service.

Read book reviews to determine if the book is one you want to read. Caution: Try to base your decision not simply on the critic's judgment (unless it is a critic you really admire), since pronouncements can vary widely.

Sign up for executive book summaries that provide subscribers with two or three 8-page book summaries every month.

Bright Idea

At the Canadian Imperial Bank of Commerce in Toronto, communications staff known as "gatekeepers" track all printed information going out to the branches, schedule distribution, edit material, and prepare a two-line synopsis of each memo and bulletin.

Look into executive tape services, which monitor about 150 publications and provide a monthly summary of top stories.

3. SKIM

"He has only half learned the art of reading who has not added to it the more refined art of skipping and skimming."

Lord Balfour, Former British Prime Minister

Skimming is what you do when you read only certain sections or segments of a book, magazine, or report rather than reading it cover to cover. Skimming helps you get though large amounts of unnecessary information quickly and focus only on those parts that are important to you.

Skimming is usually done at twice your normal reading speed, and there is a corresponding reduction in your level of comprehension. Keep in mind that skimming a magazine article or a book won't increase your understanding of it but it may give you some great ideas

One Way to Skim a Book

1. Read jacket summary information

2. Skim marketing blurbs

3. Read author profile

4. Check date of publication

5. Skim table of contents

6. Skim preface or introduction

7. Skim titles and subtitles

8. Check writing and presentation style

or interesting facts. It is easier to scroll and skim on a computer screen than it is to read on one.

We usually skim in pretty predictable patterns; however, those patterns may change depending on the topic and how familiar we are with the information.

If the book looks interesting or relevant, you can begin skimming on a more detailed level. To do this, focus on those chapters that sound particularly relevant. Begin by reading the first couple of sentences, then subheads, then the first sentence in each paragraph. When you find something that interests you, finish reading that paragraph, then read the first sentence in the next paragraph to see if you need to read that.

Unlike reading, which you must do sequentially to understand, skimming can be done by jumping all over (and is often most effective when guided by such whims). When skimming, it is important to periodically remind yourself of your goal and purpose in reading the material, since it is very easy to get sidetracked by information that is interesting but irrelevant. Allow yourself an occasional nugget of interesting information, but unless you have unlimited time to skim, make a note of the rest of the interesting information for later reading.

4. SCAN

> *People don't read today; they flip.*

John Lyons, advertising and communications writer

Scanning is similar to skimming in that you go through a large amount of information quickly. The difference is that you are looking for something in particular, whether total budget figures, time frames, or resources required. Here's the most effective way to scan information:

1. *Determine what information you are searching for.*

2. *Familiarize yourself with the content and presentation of the information,* i.e., is it arranged alphabetically or chronologically?

3. *Locate the approximate area* where you would expect to find the information, such as the letter "p" or June's sales results.

4. *Zero in on the specific information* you are looking for. Try the exercise below; find Jacob Smithers's telephone number:

Smithers Frank	943-8585
Smithers Fred	847-2733
Smithers Georgina	773-8090
Smithers Greg	329-7392
Smithers Harry	754-3718
Smithers Henry	889-4446
Smithers Ian	327-3244
Smithers Isabel	785-0900
Smithers Jackie	488-7635
Smithers Jacob	657-3226
Smithers Jason	521-4356
Smithers Larry	983-2178
Smithers Nester	774-5634

5. Search

"Knowledge is of two kinds. We know a subject ourselves, or we know where to find information upon it."

Samuel Johnson

Searching is the communication skill you need when looking for information.

1. *Identify the scope or topic of your search.* Be as clear and precise as possible about the information you need since the type and depth of information you are looking for will determine where you look. Ask for clarification

if you are not sure you understand the problem or know the goals of the project. Confusion slows you down, adds stress, and wastes effort.

If it is too early to define the scope of your search yet, you may have to embark on a "fishing expedition" to help you identify and narrow your topic.

2. *Find out if someone has already done research on the topic or project.* Do not reinvent the widget if there is already one on the market.

3. *Ask someone.* Talk to an expert in the field, or someone who has done a lot of work on a project—chances are they will be glad to talk to you and can probably suggest other good resources. Their advice could save you hours of random search time.

4. *Determine where to find the type of information you need.* Here are some of the places you might look:

Where to Find Information

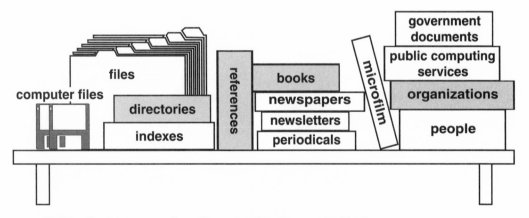

5. *Use "meta-sources,"* such as yearbooks, periodical directories, readers' abstracts, etc., to help you find out what material is available and to identify the best sources.

6. *Take advantage of a free research resource: your public library.* If you don't know how to use one, many offer orientation seminars that explain how to access and use their resources.

7. *If you are not great at organizing computer files, use operating programs (Macintosh's System 7 finder) or software capabilities ("find" or "search" on your menu).* There is also software such as Golden Retriever (Windows) or Retrieve It! (Macintosh) that can help you file and search for and within files.

8. *Subscribe to and learn how to navigate your way through an on-line service.* Service providers, such as Compuserve or Internet, will provide subscribers with access to a variety of databases for a monthly fee and usage fee. Some databases focus primarily on research, for example Dialog, which covers books and periodicals in print. Mead Data Central, Inc., offers three services: Nexis for news, Lexis for the legal profession, and Mexis for medical users.

9. *When working under a tight deadline do not get sidetracked by information that is not relevant to the current search.* File the information or make a note for future reference.

10. *If you have a research budget and are under a tight deadline, consider using professional search services,* such as Find/SVP or Info on Demand. *The Burwell Directory of Information Brokers* (formerly the *Directory of Fee-Based Information Services*), available at many libraries, contains more than 1,200 entries from 44 countries. For a fee, these experts, or "infopreneurs," offer research and document retrieval through primary and secondary sources and public and private computer databases from across the globe. Many public libraries also will conduct information searches for a fee.

11. *Know when to stop searching and when to begin evaluating and analyzing the information.*

Bright Idea[3]

At Hallmark Cards, each business unit has a fulltime "information guide"; there are currently 10 companywide. These guides are the primary point of contact for anyone at Hallmark seeking computer-based information. They translate between user information requests and the Information Management (IT) staff who can query databases and get the computerized information that users need. These guides have substantially reduced the time it takes for employees to find the right information and to compare information across business units.

12. *In addition to collecting and analyzing information, use both your professional judgment and common sense when making decisions.* Don't forget to tap into your intuition and feelings too.

13. *If the activity warrants it, hire or train special "searchers" or "guides" within your company to help employees locate corporate information.*

6. SURF

> *"A surfer takes only the barest minimum of equipment into the sea and prevails—not by opposing but by joining a wave."*
>
> George Leonard, *The Ultimate Athlete*

Surfing information is a combination of skimming, scanning, and reading, and tying all these techniques together to arrive at some level of understanding of the information.

♦ Develop the same instincts that you use to "channel-surf" on your television set. Do not judge information too quickly; keep an open mind. Stay on the surface of information, skimming and scanning, until you spot a "wave" you want to explore in more depth. Then dive in for a more detailed study.

♦ Stop viewing information as your enemy and stop fighting the raging flood. To handle a huge volume of information effectively, learn how to float with its ebbs and flows. Just like you are taught in swimming lessons, struggling only makes things worse. Remain calm and confident that you have the skills to handle it (which you will after reading this book). Manage the flood into a flow with no beginning and no end. If you can keep information flowing through your information channels, you are less likely to suffer from bottlenecks or floods.

♦ Experience information. Enjoy the sensations the experience evokes: the smell of computer paper and ink; the feeling of fingers flying over the keyboard or directing the mouse; new sights and sounds; the thrill of finding useful or interesting information or a chat group.

♦ Don't get bogged down with facts and details or obsessed with trying to memorize specific ones; this overloads your short-term memory. Instead, search for ideas and images, which are stored in long-term memory. You will need to use both parts of your brain to do this; the left hemisphere to read and logically arrange the facts and the right side to assimilate those facts and transform them into ideas. If you have any doubts about your ability to do this—perhaps after spending years in a school system that rewards rote memorization more than comprehension—do not worry. You are probably already applying this skill in other parts of your life without even being aware of it. For example, think about the way you look at a painting, not studying every brush stroke but enjoying the final picture.

Information Age Alchemy

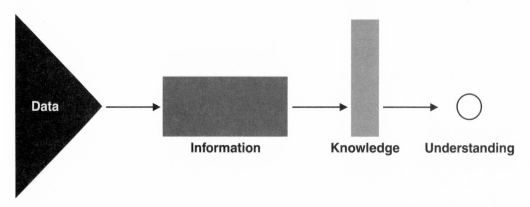

Data   **Information**   **Knowledge**   **Understanding**

♦ Become a generalist who can sift knowledge and understanding from an information flood. Think about the information to develop knowledge, and transcend your knowledge to catch a glimpse of understanding.

♦ Find patterns in what you read, see, and hear; make connections between the new information, as well as between the new information and information and knowledge already stored in your mental files. Cross-reference your mental material.

♦ Use your information tools to help you surf. With some software, you can press a key or manipulate the mouse to rearrange information in all kinds of configurations, such as by date, amount, or author. You can also easily turn lists or tables of facts and figures into charts or graphs to help you see what they mean.

7. SATISFICE

"Every general wishes he had more information before he goes into battle, but each crisis you go into is on insufficient information."

Robert Frost

As W. Russell Neuman explains in *The Future of the Mass Audience*, "satisfice" means getting just enough information to make a reasonable decision, rather than the most information to make a maximally rational choice.[4]

To stay afloat in an information flood, learn to differentiate those times when you need to base your decisions on a lot of information from those times when it is okay to "satisfice." Know when to settle for the "right" decision instead of the "best" one.

1. *Determine the decision deadline and plan research and preparation activities to meet it.* If the deadline is unrealistic or impossible, try to negotiate it.

2. *Identify the most important parts of the project or problem.* Concentrate your efforts by researching these most important aspects and seeking the best sources of information at your disposal.

3. *Do the best job possible, but don't try to be a hero all the time;* choose your victories carefully and know when being a contender is good enough. Acknowledge that you may be facing impossible deadlines and you may possess insufficient resources. Save your effort, and ulcers, for really important projects.

PRACTICE . . .THEN PRACTICE SOME MORE

Practice the seven information-receiving skills every chance you get. Though they sound simple; they are not easy. The more you practice them, the better you will become at using them.

In addition to developing the information-receiving skills, keep the following guidelines in mind.

TALK BACK

♦ Engage in proactive, assertive communication habits.

♦ Interact with information. Ask questions (even if only to yourself) or repeat the information to someone else.

♦ Send back meaningless data and reports and request clarification or ask the author to explain the relevance.

- Suggest better, more effective ways to present information to employees and colleagues. Give them a copy of this book and suggest they read Chapter 6: "Develop Information-Sending Skills."

- Fill out employee attitude and communication surveys—honestly.

- Seek out information you need and want in forms that work best for you. Seek information from a number of different sources that you trust and believe.

- Make purchasing decisions that reflect your information values and priorities, such as hiring consultants and suppliers that provide concise reports and legible invoices or by subscribing to periodicals that present information succinctly.

- Push for control and power over your own communication channels, such as that now being offered to telephone users with call display, call answer, call waiting, voice mail, etc.

- They're not listening, you say? Escalate it. Let the big boss know how you feel. To do their job, they need you to do yours, and if you are wasting a lot of time with untargeted, irrelevant information, so is your company.

READ MORE

That's right, read more and more often. Sounds kind of strange when what you are looking for is tips on how to read less? Practice will strengthen your reading skills, including speed and comprehension. In the U.S., people are reading less.[5]

> **Reality Check**
>
> If your boss, or your boss's boss is one of the main contributors to your flood, you would be wise to exercise some diplomacy when talking back. Discuss your overload problem with them—without pointing the finger directly at them—and offer suggestions. Also, explain how these changes will improve your productivity.

**Daily Newspaper
Reading (%)**

73
1967

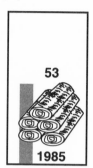
53
1985

**"Regular" Magazine
Reading (%)**

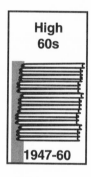
High
60s
1947-60

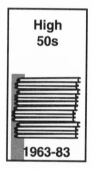
High
50s
1963-83

Book reading habits are more difficult to measure since the phrasing of the survey question has varied significantly over the years, from "Have you read a book in the past month?" to "Have you completed a book in the past month?" but this habit appears to be holding its own. "No time to read" you say?

♦ Schedule a "reading date" with yourself once a week or once a month. Read material from your "to read" file or read a good book or interesting magazine article.

♦ Take your "reading file" with you on your daily subway commute or a visit to the doctor's or dentist's office.

♦ Every couple of days, turn off the TV and pick up a good book or interesting magazine instead. (A.C. Nielsen tells us that the average adult watches about 4.5 hours of television every day.[6])

Also, read smarter. Use one of the fast, easy ways to read —read the executive summary instead of the entire report, or read just the statement of the problem and the recommendations.

REDUCE DISTRACTIONS

♦ Set aside some quiet, uninterrupted time each day—or once a week if that works better for you—to take care of heavy-duty communication tasks like reading an important report, reviewing a presentation, or analyzing a project proposal.

♦ For rush deadlines on communications projects, close your door (if you have one) and let people know that you are on deadline; place a flashing red light on your door or office baffle when a deadline is looming.

♦ If you find that your biggest problem is constant interruptions from people walking by your office or cubicle or the constant chatter going on around you, move your desk to a quieter part of the office.

♦ If you have the option, consider working at home one day a week and schedule your biggest information tasks for then.

STAY PLUGGED IN

Your computer is not the only thing that needs to be plugged in to work properly. You do too; you need to be plugged into other people. Since the mid 1960s, studies have consistently found that managers get the information they need to make decisions from the following sources:

Where Managers Get Information[7]

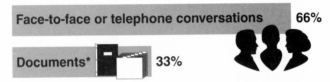

*Most external to the organization and not on the computer system

Here are some ways to plug yourself in:

♦ Transform your network into an information network. Cultivate trusted sources. Keep an eye out for relevant, important information or research findings that may interest friends and colleagues and tell them about it, or—better yet—send them a copy of it. Ask them to do the same for you. This could be an informal, ad hoc group or an official "Information Group" that meets once a month to discuss books and articles you have read.

♦ Participate in conversations. Take advantage of other people's knowledge and experience and find out what they know. One of the major benefits of face-to-face communication is that the listener can ask for clarification, ask questions, or give feedback about the information they receive. Another benefit is that people are often willing to say more informally "off the record" than they would formally "on the record." It is also easier and faster to get real, up-to-date information from a person than a piece of paper. Remember to share your information and knowledge with others too. Discussing information with others often makes that information more valuable because they can add breadth or depth or simply a different viewpoint.

♦ Subscribe to a public computing service, such as Compuserve or Prodigy, and access one or some of the electronic forums or chat groups that interest you. Share an idea or ask a question; both personal and professional friendships can develop in these forums.

♦ Pay attention to the grapevine—it can be extremely accurate. It is often more timely and specific and less filtered than official communications, including the mass media. Also, take advantage of the electronic versions of the grapevine: e-mail and the bulletin board. (Keep in mind that messages on these channels are considered business records and can be requested in a lawsuit.)

ENGAGE ALL OF YOUR SENSES

Pay attention to the messages you pick up with each of your senses. See between the lines to determine what is *not* being said. Listen to people; don't just hear what they have to say. Smell bureaucratic babble and political propaganda. Observe feelings expressed in body language—remember that 70 percent of the information in face-to-face communication comes from body language. Touch life, don't just read about it. Trust your intuition and value your experiences.

After you learn how to use the technology, learn how to use it better and faster; become a "power user."

BECOME A FRIENDLY USER

♦ Keep abreast of new technology. Take advantage of some of the new communication gadgets or software programs to help you manage your information flood. Buy the best equipment you can afford and learn how to use it properly.

Bright Idea

In Japan, large firms have formalized an informal backup communication system called the "dokikai" system. Large groups of new employees are hired at the same time and stay in touch with one another throughout their moves into different departments and climbs up the corporate ladder. Because they hang out together after hours at the local watering hole, the information they exchange is more open and honest than the official party line they exchange during business hours.[8]

♦ After you learn how to use the technology, learn how to use it better and faster; become a "power user." Learn the shortcuts and secrets of your electronic tools.

♦ Integrate some of your technology, i.e., install a fax in your computer, hook up your voice mail to your computer to record telephone messages, or implement electronic data interchange (EDI), which replaces costly paper forms with electronic documents that travel from a customer's computer to a vendor's computer and back again.

♦ Develop strong keyboarding skills so you can respond quickly.

♦ Use the technology's inherent lifesaving devices to manage information floods. These devices are the built-in capabilities of the technology such as the ability to sort e-mail messages by date, subject, or sender and the ability to skip or forward voice mail messages.

FRANK & ERNEST reprinted by permission of Newspaper Enterprise Association, Inc.

APPLY THESE SKILLS ON THE ROAD

Use technology and people to help you stay afloat in the flood from a distance.

♦ If you are on the road a lot, use a laptop, notebook, or palmtop equipped with a fax. Use a modem and telephone lines to link you to the office and company databases. Apply the same information-receiving skills you use in the office.

♦ If you do not have a secretary or the budget for mobile communication vehicles, ask two or three colleagues to monitor one of your busiest communication channels, such as your e-mail or mailbox. These monitors should regularly check that channel, respond to critical messages, and get rid of garbage and junk mail. Return the favor when they are away.

As you are getting your information flood under control, it is time to develop the information skills that will ensure you are not contributing to someone else's information flood.

REWARD CLARITY AND CONCISENESS

If you want others to send clear, concise messages, send this kind of message yourself and acknowledge their efforts when they send information in this format. Set up some kind of reward program in your department or company; it does not have to be formal or expensive.

Bright Idea

The England-based Plain English Campaign is an organization that cites companies and other organizations that have made themselves more easily understood. They also try to shame perpetuators of gobbledygook into doing better by awarding them Golden Bull Awards.

TAKE A COLD, HARD LOOK IN THE MIRROR

As you are getting your information flood under control, it is time to develop the information skills that will ensure you are not contributing to someone else's information flood.

SUMMARY

The first step in managing an information flood is to articulate your professional goals and objectives. Once you have done that, apply the seven information-receiving skills that will help you quickly and effectively filter, find, and analyze a huge quantity of information in a chaotic environment.

Many of you intuitively use some of the simpler skills, such as scanning, skimming, and surfing, to handle your flood of information. However, since few of you received any formal instruction or training for these skills, your efforts can be clumsy and ineffective.

In addition to developing the information-receiving skills, you can reduce your flood by becoming an active consumer of information instead of a passive victim and by developing a strong, informal human network to complement your electronic network.

OVERVIEW

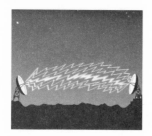

Now that you know how to manage an incoming flood of information, it is time to learn how to avoid contributing to anyone else's flood.

Whereas a flood is an act of nature, an information flood is an act of humans, their environment, and their tools. However, often we have the power and skills to reduce or minimize both types of floods.

This chapter outlines the seven skills needed by those who send information to prevent or reduce information floods.

DEVELOP INFORMATION-SENDING SKILLS

*Communicate unto the other guy that which
you would want him to communicate unto you
if your positions were reversed.*

Aaron Goldman
CEO, The Macke Company
(Sign given to all managers)

6

ACKNOWLEDGE YOUR CONTRIBUTION TO THE GLUT

Unless you answer "yes" to most of the questions in the following quiz, the next step in managing an information flood is to admit that you are contributing to it. (Remember the "Common Culprits" from Chapter 4?) Isn't it funny how everyone complains of suffering from information overload, but few of us acknowledge that we contribute to the flood.

Take the following self-quiz . . . if you dare.

Are You a Skilled Information Sender?

	Yes	No	Not Sure
I always keep my audience in mind when I send information.			
I have strong written and oral communication skills and apply them to whichever media I use.			
I am constantly taking courses or reading books to strengthen my basic communication skills and to develop new information-sending skills.			
I work to get my audience's attention and to make my messages stand out.			
I am a well-rounded communicator who knows how to show, not tell, my message.			
I never dump data. I always explain what the data means.			
I know how to communicate dynamic, constantly changing information.			
I separate critical information from the chaotic for my audience.			
I present information in quick and easy-to-read formats.			
I choose the most appropriate media for my audience and my message.			
I know when I have said enough and I don't say any more.			

After you've completed this quiz, give it to some of the people you send information to and ask them to complete it about your information skills. You may be surprised at the discrepancy between your perception of your skills and your audience's perception of them. You may also want to observe and record your sending habits by completing the "Outgoing Information" chart in the Appendix.

> ## Business Writing Principles[1]
>
> 1. No one wants to read it.
>
> 2. Almost no one will read all of it.
>
> 3. Almost everyone will misunderstand some part of it.

MEMORIZE THE THREE BUSINESS WRITING PRINCIPLES

These principles aren't meant to discourage you, but to help you recognize the obstacles you will face as you try to communicate with someone in the business world. Though these guidelines were designed specifically for writing, they also apply to other information media.

THINK ABOUT WHAT YOU ARE DOING

Though the deadline is fast approaching and you must communicate quickly, slow down for a moment. Think about what you are doing and why you are doing it.

Do you want to inform your audience about something, or are you trying to persuade them to do something? Your objective will not only determine the what and how of the message, but also the best information channel for transmission.

Resist the tendency to automatically create a written document and send it to everyone. Maybe a face-to-face chat or an

> ### You Said It[2]
>
> "What organization men say or write or print means nothing at all, being merely the bureaucratic equivalent of breaking wind. To succeed in the art of communication, we have to make a big effort of imagination. We have to put ourselves in the position of the people we seek to influence...to see the situation from their point of view. This is the most difficult task of all."

informal e-mail would serve your purpose better. Or maybe you have nothing to say that your audience wants to hear.

KNOW YOUR AUDIENCE

Most of us write for our favorite audience: ourselves. We like the sound of our own voice and are impressed with our writing ability. Unfortunately, most of the information we send goes to other people. We must learn to write for other audiences.

When sending information, know who your audience is and what kind of information it needs. To start, make sure you address the *right* audience and the *whole* audience. How often have you attended a project meeting where you talked to the senior manager of a department first and then had to repeat everything to the person who is going to actually do the work?

If you are communicating to only one person or a few people that you know personally, customize the message for their needs, interests, and, ideally, even their personalities. For example, are they "bottom-line" types who want you to get to the point right away, or are they more sociable and thus appreciative of a few personal comments before getting down to business?

In communicating to a larger audience, it is impossible to customize the message or to consider individual preferences and personalities. There are, however, a few guidelines to keep in mind about business audiences:[3]

- ◆ They are very conscious of organizational hierarchies, so you must be credible.

- ◆ They tend to be interested in the bottom line versus abstract concepts.

- ◆ Because they are action-oriented, they tend to prefer solutions to problems.

♦ Like every other audience, they are interested in their own concerns, not yours. Ensure that you tell them how your proposal will affect them.

As a general rule of thumb, **senior managers and executives** need broad coverage that results from analysis, synthesis, and evaluation. They also need access to the details, if they decide they want to see something in greater depth. **Mid-level managers** need more detailed information and narrower coverage. **First-line supervisors** need information that will help them fulfill their operating responsibilities.

BALANCE THE AUDIENCE'S NEEDS WITH YOURS

As the information sender, you have certain things you need or want to say. Your audience, on the other hand, has certain things that they need or want to hear. Your job is to marry the two often conflicting demands.

One way to achieve the necessary balance is to have your internal reader help your internal writer communicate. No one likes to read government or business style writing, but almost everyone writes it. Your reader knows when to stop; it is your long-winded writer that goes on and on . . . and on . . . and on.

DEVELOP THE SEVEN INFORMATION-SENDING SKILLS

In today's fast-paced business world, with thousands of messages competing for an audience's attention, you need to develop seven skills to send information effectively. These skills can be applied to all media from written memos to voice mail messages to presentations.

Information-Sending Skills	
1. Seduce	Grab your reader's attention. Ensure your objective for sending the information is achieved.
2. Synthesize	Draw all relevant information together, analyze it, and explain it for your audience.
3. Show	Use graphic elements and "visual words" to convey your message.
4. Sort	Present information in an easy-to-receive, flexible style that allows the recipient to handle it quickly and easily.
5. Separate	Separate critical information from that which is simply chaotic, and communicate both effectively.
6. Select	Choose the right information channel for the type of information you are sending and for your purpose in sending it.
7. Stay silent	Know when you have said enough or have nothing to say, and say no more.

1. SEDUCE

"I can resist everything except temptation."

Oscar Wilde

Seducing is the art of grabbing your audience's attention. You have about thirty seconds to convince your audience to read or look at your message while competing with dozens of other messages and priorities. You also have to cut through reception barriers, such as stress, defensiveness, and resistance to change.

♦ Ensure your message will make it to the recipient's screening. To do this, your message must be valuable, useful, important, relevant, or interesting to the person receiving it.

♦ The most obvious way to grab a reader's attention is to use compelling, specific, unique, informative titles or headlines. Create titles that reflect the message for the reader. Over the years, I have received dozens of e-mails that list the subject as "No Subject" or "Document 946759999030"— neither of which is particularly inviting.

♦ After your title, your first, or "lead," sentence is the next item that will determine whether your message sinks or swims. Its purpose is to draw the reader into the article, document, or report.

♦ Seduce your audience beyond the first sentence. Make the document inviting and easy to read with creative presentation techniques and interesting graphic elements. Use a legible typeface, short paragraphs, lots of white space, subheadings, bullets, bold words, underlining, etc.

♦ It is easier to seduce your audience when you use devices that save time for both you and them, such as executive summaries, overviews, highlights, synopses, templates, and standardized formats. Many word processing programs include a selection of "express" documents, such as letters, forms, FAX cover letters, memos, slides, and borders.

2. SYNTHESIZE

"When you're facing a fire hydrant of information, someone who can hand you a glass of water will become very important."

Mitch Kapor
founder, Lotus Development Corp.

Synthesizing is the skill of collecting all relevant information, analyzing, and explaining it to your audience. Information should not be a puzzle that recipients have to put together—most have neither the time nor the inclination to do that. It is the sender's job to put the puzzle together before sending the information.

Political Pros[4]

Like Reagan and Thatcher, Ontario premier Mike Harris used television as a political tool during his campaign, setting up scenes that connected his policies to simple images:

He unveiled a flatbed truck with 31 chairs to show how many seats at the legislature were not needed. The truck then drove away from the legislature. He unveiled a sign announcing a town called Welfare, Ontario, Population 1,300,00. Viewers get the point that welfare recipients make up an entire city.

♦ Research your topic. Draw together all relevant observations, facts, figures, analyses, and evaluations.

♦ Provide a context for information and analyze data. Do not just do a "data dump." For example, instead of just announcing that the company is cutting $3 million from its administrative budget, indicate what percentage of the total budget that represents and outline what the cut will mean to employees and customers. Also, suggest solutions or alternatives, such as teleconferencing instead of traveling or a bulk discount for office supplies from a new supplier. Clearly outline any necessary actions and the appropriate steps.

♦ Find out if anyone is working on a similar project and combine your reports or presentations—the goal is less, more comprehensive information.

3. SHOW

"A picture is worth a thousand words."

Or put another way, a picture is worth approximately eight minutes of talking or two pages of text. Showing is the skill of presenting information either verbally—with metaphors, analogies, and symbols—or visually—with pictures and diagrams—to help your audience see what you are saying.

Showing information instead of simply telling it makes it colorful and memorable. It is also more inviting and easier to read than pages of text or hours of talking.

Which Would You Rather Receive?

Revenues
(000)

	Forecast	Actual
January	17,462	16,935
February	18,967	18,392
March	18,142	12,291
April	17,324	19,739
May	19,893	17,045
June	18,502	18,885

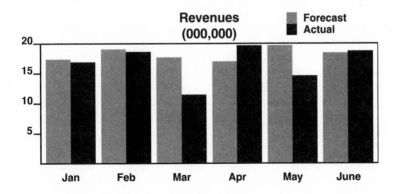

Besides the bar chart, other common forms of visual communication include diagrams, drawings, photographs, computer graphics, and the visuals below:

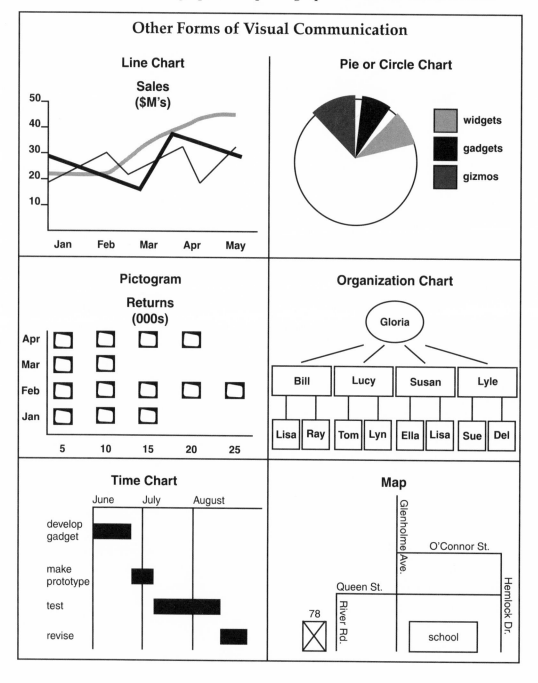

Other Forms of Visual Communication

Line Chart
Sales ($M's)

Pie or Circle Chart
widgets
gadgets
gizmos

Pictogram
Returns (000s)

Organization Chart
Gloria — Bill, Lucy, Susan, Lyle
Lisa, Ray, Tom, Lyn, Ella, Lisa, Sue, Del

Time Chart
develop gadget
make prototype
test
revise

Map
Glenholme Ave., O'Connor St., Queen St., River Rd., Hemlock Dr., school, 78

"Showing" is becoming increasingly important with the growth of multimedia and other visual information technology. For example, you can now attach a video to reports or include a roving cartoon character in presentations.

To maintain your credibility, show the whole picture and not simply a snapshot of one small area. A good visualization paints the big picture and shows relationships. Also, ensure that analogies and metaphors are appropriate for your information. However, do not overdo the graphics or use them indiscriminately since this can look tacky or be confusing. The goal is to enhance your message, not bury it.

4. SORT

The writer does the most who gives
his reader the most knowledge and takes from
him the least time."

Charles Caleb Colton
English cleric, sportsman, and wine merchant,
Lacon

Sorting is the skill of presenting information in an easy-to-receive, flexible style. When sending information, sort it so it can be read, skimmed, scanned, or surfed in a variety of ways depending on the audiences' needs and preferences.

One of the most effective ways of sorting information is into varying degrees of detail so your audience can access as much or as little as they need. Start with a title, then a summary, the entire article or report divided into manageable and meaningful chunks, background information, further references, and finally statistical tables.

You Choose[5]

In 1987, GTE spent six weeks and less than $14,000 creating a Hypercard system that lets executives keep up on how the company's many business units are doing. With the system, an executive can pick a figure from a table and with a click get the backup for it. Clicking on monthly sales for a region might bring up a bar chart that breaks sales down by product categories. The system is also programmed with a set of figures that represent acceptable business performance, so it can flag numbers that deviate.

Sort large amounts of information into smaller sections that are logical, quick to read, and easy to find. When working on a $22 million budget cut that included 36 different initiatives, we identified half a dozen major trends, such as administrative cuts, prioritizing work, reducing sponsorships, etc., and grouped the initiatives under the appropriate subheading.

5. SEPARATE

It is not the quantity but the pertinence [of your words] that does the business.

Seneca, Roman writer and rhetorician

Separate critical information from that which is merely chaotic.

In today's chaotic, complex environment, you must often quickly communicate information that is constantly changing. To do this you must shift from literate to post-literate communication skills, as indicated on the following chart.

Separate and highlight critical information from that which is merely chaotic by using a special communication channel or warning signal.

General Guidelines for Crisis Communication

1. Create a crisis communication channel (or channels) in your organization, such as an e-mail flash that immediately appears on the recipient's screen accompanied by a loud, distinctive sound, a special "Red Alert" memo, a printed report, or a distinctive telephone ring. If all the people who need to be informed and involved are geographically close, hold face-to-face meetings or work together on the crisis in the same room.

Communication Skills for Chaotic Environments

	Literate	Post-literate
Nature of Communication	static, rigid	dynamic, flexible
Speed	however long it took to produce and distribute	instantaneous
Favorite Form(s)	written	e-mail, voice mail, verbal, written
Sender's Role	waits for information to come to them	aggressively searches for information; cultivates numerous sources
Recipient's Role	passive	interactive
Content	answers, decisions, solutions, results	questions, problems, approaches, plans
Tone	formal	informal
Bias	selected facts—what, when, where—fudged by political agendas	all relevant facts with explanations and reasons
Logic	linear, detail-rich	circular, big-picture focus
Impetus	written for self or boss	written for audience
Who Controls It	sender	recipient—they choose topics and degree of detail through menus, hypertext, or databases
Sign-off	numerous approvals	maximum one approval

2. Keep your crisis channel simple and ensure that it is confidential.

3. When developing your crisis channel, ensure that it always overrides recipients' screening systems.

4. Ensure that everyone who needs to have a crisis channel or access to one has it. Critical messages should go to more than one person but fewer than twelve. (It can go to an unlimited number of people as an FYI item.)

5. Develop criteria for what type of information should be sent on the crisis channel and ensure that all participants are aware of these guidelines. Use your crisis channel to flag real emergencies only. Don't include information that is simply "important" or "urgent." Expect some people to abuse the system (especially at first), but take steps to reduce this abuse. If you abuse and overuse the crisis channel, recipients will start to ignore it and the channel will lose its effectiveness.

For example, if you created a crisis channel for health and safety issues, you would not want people cluttering the channel with information on the number of absentees last month, stress reduction tips, or replacement pages for a procedures manual. You would only want the channel used to alert recipients to a major gas leak, medical emergency, product recall, etc.

6. Develop feedback rules that outline when the recipient(s) must get back to the sender with an action plan. Develop time lines that are realistic and effective. Ensure they are followed. If not, have someone follow up to find out why not.

7. Develop a system that allows people to send crisis information directly, rather than having it filtered, massaged, and mangled by five different levels of management. Limit any necessary approvals to one, even if that means CEO sign-off.

8. Develop distribution lists for your crisis channel ahead of time, such as all members of a special project or key company executives. Keep the lists up-to-date.

9. During a crisis, keep your audiences well-informed. Provide them with status reports as soon as you have them. Stick to the facts. Be honest about what you do and do not know.

10. If you have more than one crisis channel operating at the same time, differentiate between them and rate them according to importance.

11. Develop crisis plans for major potential problems, including contingency plans for each before the emergency. A crisis is no time to absorb information or decide how to act on that information. The crisis channel is designed to transmit the information that will set off one of the contingency plans and keep everyone who needs to know informed of developments.

6. SELECT

"He who has choice has trouble."

Dutch proverb

Select is the skill of choosing the best communication channel for your message. With all the communication channels available today, it is easy to resort to the easiest or fastest channel; however, different media are best for different types of information. When selecting the media, consider the following factors:

♦ Audience access to technology

♦ Channels receivers feel most comfortable using

♦ Formality of your message

♦ Type or purpose of your information

♦ Action you need or expect from your audience

♦ Urgency and importance of your message

Inherent advantages and disadvantages of the most popular communication channels follow:

Pros and Cons of Written Communication[6]

+	-
◆ Receiver must take an active role in the communication process	◆ Needs more time to send their message
◆ Effectiveness depends on reader's ability and interest, as well as writer's skill	◆ Needs spelling, punctuation, and other mechanical skill
◆ Reading is faster than listening—you can read 3-5 times more than you could hear in an hour	◆ No immediate feedback
◆ Writing is less personal	◆ Less personal, more one-dimensional
◆ Writing provides a permanent record	◆ Receiver is in control—can easily choose not to read the message
◆ Writing can be revised	

Pros and Cons of Oral Communication[7]
(Including face-to-face and presentations)

+	-
◆ Fast—average person speaks at a rate of about 150 words/minute	**Originate With Speaker**
◆ Fewer mechanical problems, i.e., grammar, punctuation, spelling	◆ Dress and appearance
◆ Greater degree of vitality and flexibility than written forms	◆ Nervous delivery
◆ Speaker's voice and body language add meaning and variety	◆ Inaudible or unpleasant voice
◆ Allows feedback from the receiver	◆ Extraneous noise, i.e., jewelry, shuffling paper
◆ More personal—emphasizes the human element in communication	◆ Different accent
◆ Spontaneous	◆ Lack of eye contact or too much eye contact (a sign of hostility)
	◆ Distracting mannerisms
	◆ Too much detail for audience
	Originate With Hearer
	◆ Inability to hear
	◆ Physical distractions, i.e., discomfort, fatigue
	◆ Negative attitude toward speaker
	◆ Paying attention to something in room rather than speaker
	◆ Daydreaming
	◆ Lack of background information on topic
	◆ Cannot understand speaker's vocabulary
	◆ Speaking to someone else
	◆ Taking notes

Pros and Cons of Telephone

+	-
♦ Fast, cheap, universal	♦ Loss of visual cues about your audience's environment, data about their feelings and emotions, nonverbal language gestures
♦ Simple to use	
♦ Immediate, two-way	
♦ Informal, personal channel	
♦ All telephones are compatible	♦ Loss of control over environment, such as noise, interruptions, etc.
	♦ May get voice mail system rather than person
	♦ No record of discussions or decisions
	♦ Easy to get off topic or to chat
	♦ Time of call may not be mutually convenient

Pros and Cons of Voice Mail

+	-
◆ Ends telephone tag	◆ Some people use it as an electronic shield or screen
◆ Allows message to get to your audience	◆ Difficult to leave lengthy or detailed messages
◆ Can transmit emotion better than e-mail or fax	◆ Easy for recipients to transpose numbers
◆ Allows others to get your message when they need it, in spite of different time zones or a person's absence	◆ Limits on message storage capacity and time
◆ Messages tend to be shorter, more direct than memos or telephone calls	◆ No selective retrieval of messages
◆ Same message can be sent to many people simultaneously	◆ Cannot retrieve a voice mail message once you have sent it
◆ Messages can be stored electronically	◆ Deleting a message does not mean that it is gone; the system may have saved it
◆ Easily accessed off-site with a touch-tone telephone	

Pros and Cons of E-Mail (Electronic Mail)

+	-
◆ You can sort messages by receiver, date or subject	◆ On some systems you cannot retrieve a message once you have sent it
◆ Copies can be sent to a number of other people	◆ Ability to respond immediately can lead to overreacting or "flaming" — sending an angry or negative response
◆ Messages can easily be forwarded	
◆ Crosses time zones without having to wake up others	
◆ Can send a reply that contains the original message	◆ Requires strong, basic writing skills
◆ Receipt file can let you know when someone opens your message	◆ Often reduces or replaces face-to-face communication
◆ Tends to be employees favorite communication channel	◆ Audience may have incompatible systems
◆ Fast, convenient, simple to use	◆ Those who are not on the system or who aren't competent with it will feel left out
◆ Tone tends to be informal, conversational, friendly	
◆ More tolerant of spelling and grammatical errors than formal written channels	◆ Easy to overuse; if everyone sends "urgent" messages, overuse will diminish the sense of urgency
◆ Messages are short	◆ Can't guarantee confidentiality; you could hit the wrong button and send it to the wrong person or someone could read it when it is sent to the printer. It can also be forwarded to others
◆ Easy to ignore protocols and ignore hierarchies	
◆ It is a direct medium; employees can access anyone they wish	
◆ Paperless, but you can leave a paper trail, if necessary	◆ Deleting a message doesn't mean it's gone; it may have been backed up on the system
◆ Can leave detailed messages	
◆ Can attach files from word-processing programs or spreadsheets	
◆ Messages can be stored electronically in folders	

Pros and Cons of Fax Machine

+	-
♦ Convenient	♦ Paper-based
♦ Easy to plug in and simple to use	♦ Junk faxes are common
♦ Inexpensive	♦ Difficult to get through busy lines
♦ Just about everyone has one, and they're all compatible	♦ Sensitive or confidential information must be handled with care
♦ Fastest way to send paper, i.e., reports, graphs, maps, etc.	♦ Can't be stored electronically for later changes
♦ Can receive data with little or no attention from anyone in the office (other than ensuring there's enough paper)	♦ May tie up telephone line if you only have one line
♦ Can serve as a permanent record, unlike voice mail	♦ Best used with less than 10 pages
	♦ Depending on your distribution system, it may not be delivered promptly
	♦ Must confirm receipt if document is really important or urgent

Pros and Cons of Audioconference
(a telephone call where more than two
people are connected)

+	-
♦ Convenient (can communicate any time from any location) ♦ Economical, cuts down on business travel ♦ Saves time; eliminates need to travel ♦ Reliable ♦ Efficient; participants stick to agenda, make decisions, and are more aware of time	♦ Loss of visual cues about your audience's environment and about feelings and emotions shown through body language ♦ Loss of control over environment, such as noise, interruptions ♦ Someone using a speaker phone is hard to interrupt

Pros and Cons of Videoconferencing
(TV and voice systems designed for conference use)

+	-
♦ Convenient (can communicate any time from any location) ♦ Economical, cuts down on business travel ♦ Saves time; eliminates the need to travel ♦ Reliable ♦ Efficient; participants stick to agenda, make decisions, and are more aware of time	♦ Choppy video images ♦ Synchronization of sound and picture may be off ♦ Delays when including data and documents ♦ Traditional boardroom style (as opposed to PC version) is expensive and inflexible ♦ Some people are intimidated by the camera and freeze

Pros and Cons of Multimedia
(A computer-based communication tool that uses several media at once including text, video, voice, sound effects, and music. It is generally interactive with viewers controlling what they see and hear.)

+	-
♦ Audience retains information better when they can see and hear it, even more when they can interact with it ♦ Especially effective for training ♦ Can be reused, reproduced, and modified at little additional cost	♦ Expensive and time-consuming to produce professional quality ♦ Audience must have access to the same system as you, and must be willing to upload a disk ♦ Real danger of going overboard with special effects because they're so easy to create

Hypertext
(Presents information in a format that lets the user jump easily from topic to topic, or to drill deeper for more detail)

+	-
♦ Same benefits of interactivity as multimedia ♦ Less expensive and time-consuming to produce professional quality than multimedia ♦ Branching ability provides shortcuts to information not available to conventional hierarchical databases ♦ Audience can choose depth and direction they want to explore ♦ Can easily and quickly navigate through lots of information	♦ Requires compatible systems and software

Pros and Cons of the Internet

+	-
◆ Can share valuable information with people in several locations	◆ Still relatively crude and rudimentary
◆ Possible to connect with others who share your interests	◆ Requires specialized knowledge
◆ No central rule-making authority	◆ Difficult to navigate
◆ Access to vast pool of information	◆ Slow because not designed for volume of data it contains
	◆ Contains lots of useless information
	◆ Decentralized and disorganized
	◆ No quality control

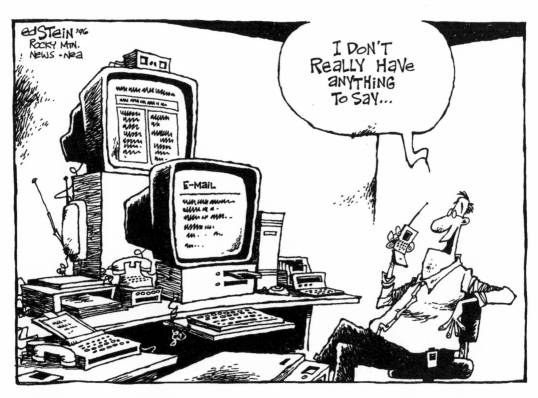

ED STEIN reprinted by permission of Newspaper Enterprise Association, Inc.

7. STAY SILENT

*"To talk too much and arrive nowhere
is the same as climbing a tree
to catch a fish."*

Chinese proverb

The most important information-sending skill is knowing when you have nothing more to say . . . and saying nothing more. Other ways to cut down on the noise include the following:

♦ Use "exception reporting" to communicate regular information, such as quarterly reports. Exception reporting is reporting exceptions or significant increases or decreases from standard results, (amount predetermined) or positive or negative trends.

♦ Consider producing regular reports less often, say monthly instead of weekly. Combine reports.

KEEP IT SIMPLE

In addition to the seven information-sending skills outlined previously, there are a number of other actions you can take to reduce your contribution to the information flood.

Get to the point quickly and communicate the rest of your message just as fast. Remember that your goal is to express, not to impress with your vocabulary or wit.

♦ Tell readers why you are writing to them and, if you need them to do something, explain what that is in specific detail. Outline the urgency of your request—"We're getting a

Bright Idea[8]

Siegal & Gale Ltd. of Cambridge, England, an information design company, redesigned the Dutch government's inland revenue forms. The new tax returns weigh less than their predecessors, are easier to complete, and saved the government nearly $5 million in postage and processing charges. Siegal & Gale also reduced the British Mental Health Act from 140 pages of text to a simple flow chart for UK social workers.

lot of customer complaints on Product X and need some new tests conducted by Friday, October 6."

Some companies use "action memos" or customized Post-it™ Notes when distributing information. These useful tools have 10-20 different actions the sender can tick off to tell the receiver exactly what he or she is supposed to do with the information. An example follows:

```
                      MEMO

❏ FYI                    ❏ As per our discussion
❏ Note and file          ❏ As per your request
❏ Note and return to me  ❏ Return for my approval
❏ Note and see me        ❏ Return with more details
❏ Work assignment        ❏ Return with comments
❏ For your approval      ❏ Returned with thanks
❏ Investigate and report ❏ Initial, circulate, and return
❏ Take appropriate action ❏ _____
```

♦ Limit the number of messages in a single memo or document to two or three.

♦ Simplify messages. Make them crystal clear.

♦ Use deductive, not inductive writing; state your conclusion first and then give the explanations or reasons for it. (The only exception is when you are communicating a negative message or trying to persuade your audience to think or do something—at these times you may want to open with a buffer.)

REDUCE DISTRACTIONS

Set aside some quiet, uninterrupted time each day, or once a week if that works better for you, specifically to take care of intensive information-sending tasks, such as writing a report, preparing a presentation, or developing a project proposal.

TAKE ADVANTAGE OF YOUR TOOLS

Learn how to use your hardware and software to research, compile, and present information, succinctly and effectively. For example, most word-processing programs allow you to create bulleted lists, tables, or columns quickly and easily.

SIGN UP FOR A GOOD COMMUNICATION COURSE

The Good Old Days[9]

When an engineer at Intel Corporation in Santa Clara, California, wanted a $2.79 mechanical pencil, processing the order used to require 12 pieces of paper and 95 administrative steps...In 1979 the company began an attack on its own bureaucracy that makes it possible today for the company to get those pencils with only one form and eight steps.

When is the last time you took a communications course? In high school? College? In the Information Age, the concept of lifelong learning is especially applicable to communication and information-management skills. Seek training on both hard and soft communication skills. Keep your eyes open for courses that will help you develop new or different communication skills.

Soft communication skills include planning ahead (instead of always putting out fires), articulating purpose, setting objectives, thinking, developing strategies and tactics, identifying audiences, and evaluating results.

Hard skills include not only writing, reading, speaking, and grammar, but also research, graphic design, layout, presentation, and keyboarding or typing skills. The two main benefits of improving your typing are relevance—more technology requires it—and speed—typing is at least twice as fast as handwriting.

Flying Fingers[10]

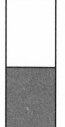

40-45 words per minute is the average typing speed (Possible even for a poor typist)

Less than 20 words per minute is the regular handwriting speed

READ MORE

The more you read, the better you will write. Also, the higher the quality of what you read, the better the quality of your writing. Voracious readers tend to be good writers.[11] The reason is the sound of words; reading a lot gives you knowledge of the sound of the language in its written form, and that knowledge helps you to write well. Also, reading is a painless way to develop an awareness of basic language mechanics, such as punctuation, spelling, grammar, and usage. This knowledge gets rusty fast, but regular reading helps to sharpen your sense of how writing mechanics work even when you cannot remember grammatical terms or rules.

PRACTICE

Like most other skills, practice will make you a better information sender. It is also a good idea to develop different communications skills for different information channels, such as letters and memos, presentations, and friendly e-mail messages.

Evaluate Your Information

Stop asking whether people liked the color of a brochure or the typeface you used in a report—find out what they learned from it or what they did as a result of reading it. Measure the success of your information on the ease and speed with which your audience comprehend it. Work to develop areas of weakness.

Summary

To ensure that your messages are getting through the clutter, the first step is to acknowledge that every time you send a memo, distribute a report, or fire off an e-mail to the entire office, you are probably contributing to someone else's information flood.

As an information sender, you need to learn how to target your messages to the right audience(s), grab and hold their attention, communicate those messages succinctly and meaningfully, and choose the right communication channel for the message and its purpose. You also need to stop thinking of yourself only as a writer and develop other, post-literate communication skills, such as effectively communicating constantly changing information and communicating visuals as well as words.

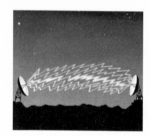

OVERVIEW

Now that you have learned how to develop the attitudes and skills to more effectively manage both incoming and outgoing information, it is time to learn how to ensure that you do not drown again.

Information flood control involves

♦ Prevention—paying attention to warning signals, familiarizing yourself with your surroundings, and listening to forecasts, i.e., knowing a large flood of information will follow your division's reorganization

♦ Maintenance—regularly cleaning information channels and keeping them free of debris

This chapter outlines some of the common obstacles and relapse traps faced by those attempting to deal with information overload. It also offers suggestions on how to overcome or avoid these obstacles and traps.

Don't Fall in Again

The inflow of information and intelligence...
has long since passed the point of digestibility.

Stephan K. Bailey, President, American Society
of Public Administration

7

A good general suggestion to help maintain your resolve and commitment to *InfoRelief* is to regularly remind yourself of the value of managing an information flood. To refresh your memory, refer to the benefits listed in the first chapter.

Another good idea is to celebrate your achievements, both large and small. In an information flood, it is very easy to focus only on what still needs to be done while ignoring all you have achieved. During particularly turbulent times, you could remind yourself that if you do not manage your information flood it will control you by increasing your workload and stress levels.

Following are the most common obstacles that may hinder your ability to manage your information flood and the relapse traps you may encounter. There are also suggestions on how to overcome them both.

You say . . .	I say . . .
"I don't know where to start."	"Of course you do. You've already started by reading this book. Approach your information tasks one step at a time. Start by applying one or two of the simpler skills. Give yourself some time to clean out the information currently clogging your channels. Set small goals. Don't expect it all to disappear overnight.
"I don't have enough time."	Make the time. Make information-handling tasks a priority: Ironically, it will give you more time by helping you become more productive and effective. Also, don't forget to delegate some of your information tasks.
"I've got more important things to do."	Then do them. When crises eclipse information tasks, keep up a basic level of maintenance and let the rest slide. Recommit to your information tasks the minute the crisis has passed and you have had a chance to recuperate. Using the *InfoRelief* skills will give you more time for true crises.

You say . . .	I say . . .
"I'll do it tomorrow."	There will be more information to manage tomorrow. Get started today and you will have less to do. Set yourself a deadline for the first small step . . . then set a deadline for the next small step.
"The old ways were easier."	That may be, but were they effective? With time, the new ways will become easier too. By all means keep those skills and habits that worked and simply integrate some of the new skills into your system.
"I'm not good at this kind of stuff."	You don't have to do all your information tasks perfectly the first time you do them. There are probably several skills you will pick up very quickly. Practice will improve the rest.
"I've done it perfectly for a week, but I can't keep it up."	Double-check your information goals and make sure they are realistic. Balance information tasks with other work. Recognize that Herculean efforts are doomed to eventual failure. Some information tasks, such as dealing with junk mail, can be dealt with on automatic pilot.

You say . . .	I say . . .
"I've got it all under control."	Congratulations, but don't be lulled into believing that you don't need to do anything more. Information overload is not a problem to be fixed, but a process to be managed. As new technologies develop and current ones expand, the same problems will need to be addressed again and again.
"People are giving me a hard time for trying to get some InfoRelief."	Have patience. Be firm in your resolve to stay afloat in the information flood but don't force others before they are ready. Lead by example; change yourself before asking others to change. Suggest solutions; emphasize the benefits of managing the flood instead of focusing on problems or people's weaknesses.

Summary

Managing an information flood is an ongoing process, not a one-time project. The process can be difficult, and you may face many challenges and obstacles. Circumvent the inevitable rough water by being realistic about what you can and cannot achieve, recognizing the value of managing your information and being flexible in handling the ebbs and flows of your workload.

Sales manager Jacob Smithers strolls into his office early Monday morning after spending a four-day long weekend relaxing up at his cottage. (He was disturbed only once with an urgent, important telephone call from the office).

He closes his office door and call forwards his telephone to his voice mail system. When he sits down at his desk and logs onto his electronic mail system, he finds 32 messages with the 14 urgent or important messages prioritized according to source and topic at the top. One of the messages is from a colleague and it has a one-page attachment: a flow chart of the department's new re-engineering plan. After quickly responding to all of the messages or adding tasks to today's "to do" list, Jacob deletes or files them. He then accesses and scans the bulletin board to check out new postings and sees changes to an accounting policy that he deals with almost daily. He transfers the four new pages into the hypertext version of his accounting binder.

Out of the corner of his eye, he sees a half-inch pile of paper. When he turns his head in that direction he sees his mail from the last few days: the pile contains 12 letters and memos (thanks to an internal directive, the 9 internal memos are all one page long and begin with a one paragraph synopsis of the content), 2 magazines, and 1 newsletter. He skims each of the letters and memos; reads 2 in more detail, files 1, delegates 2, and trashes 7.

He then quickly skims the newsletter, reads one article, and tears out another and adds it to his "read on the subway" file. Four 1-page sales reports sit next to this pile of new paper; 3 are executive summaries with a notation on where to access the entire report, and 1 is an exception report with a chart illustrating changes from last month's results. A handwritten note on top informs

Jacob that the reports will be discussed at tomorrow's staff meeting. As he begins reading the reports and scribbling his notes directly on each page, a loud beep from his computer draws his attention to the screen where he sees a meeting notice from the national sales director informing him of an emergency meeting at 10:00 a.m. this morning. His computer system automatically schedules the meeting for him as he finishes reviewing the reports and puts them away for tomorrow's meeting. His system will remind him of the meeting at 9:45.

At that point, the group's secretary knocks on the door and walks into his office. After welcoming him back from his vacation, she hands him 4 faxes and informs him that he is not scheduled to attend any other meetings today—the only urgent matter is being dealt with in a one-hour conference call this afternoon. As Jacob contemplates this flow of information, he's glad he and his wife listened to the taped executive summaries of 6 popular business books on the trips to and from the cottage over the weekend. He types a note into his calendar reminding him to stop at the bookstore during lunch to pick up another copy of *InfoRelief* to send to a friend in Germany. Feeling calm and well-rested after his mini-holiday, Jacob reaches for the candy in the top drawer of his desk. He munches a couple of jellybeans. Spotting the flashing light on his telephone, he picks up the receiver and punches in his access code. An electronic-sounding voice informs him that he has 3 new messages waiting. He listens to the urgent one first and immediately sends a response to the caller's voice mail. He listens to the first sentence of the second one and skips the rest of the message since he already discussed the matter with the caller at the water cooler this morning. After listening to the third message, he jots another task on his "to do" list. He deletes each voice mail message after listening to it.

Jacob hangs up the phone, hesitates for a moment and then picks it up again and dials his home number.

When his wife answers, he tells her that he is looking forward to going to the theater tonight to see the new play that has been getting such good reviews. He suggests they meet before the show for dinner at their favorite Chinese restaurant across from the theater. After hanging up, Jacob gets up from his desk and opens his office door just as a colleague arrives for the day. After greeting each other, they chat about the sloppy playing of a highly paid outfielder during Sunday's baseball game.

Appendix

Incoming information

when	who	where	channel	topic	purpose	my response	why	reaction

Outgoing information

when	who	where	channel	topic	purpose	response

Notes

CHAPTER 1: ARE YOU DROWNING?

1. Government red tape costs $166 billion/year—Albert Crenshaw, "Battle Looms Over Renewal of Federal Paperwork Reduction Act," *Washington Post* (September 11, 1989), p. WB6.

2. Christopher Burns, "Three Mile Island: The Information Meltdown" in *Great Information Disasters* by Dr. Forst W. Horton, Jr., and Dr. Dennis Lewis, The Association for Information Management, Silver Spring, Maryland, 1991, pp. 45-54.

CHAPTER 2: WHAT CAUSES INFORMATION OVERLOAD?

1. 60 billion faxes—Stephen Barr, "Fax Boards Are Supplement Not Fax Machine Replacement," *Crain's New York Business* (April 29, 1991), p. 26.

2. Cheryl Currid, *Electronic Invasion. Brave New World of Business Communications,* Brady Computer Books, New York, 1993, p. 144.

3. Transition not complete until 2010 or 2020—Peter Drucker, "The New Society of Organizations," *Harvard Business Review* (September/October 1992), p. 96.

4. M. Salter, "Plug and Pray," *Globe & Mail* (Report on Business Magazine) (March 1995).

5. 60 billion faxes—Stephen Barr, "Fax Boards Are Supplement Not Fax Machine Replacement," *Crain's New York Business* (April 29, 1991), p. 26.

6. Peter Large, *The Micro Revolution Revisited,* Rowman & Allenheld, Lanham, Maryland, 1984, p. 46.

7. Peter Large, *The Micro Revolution Revisited,* Rowman & Allenheld, Lanham, Maryland, 1984, p. 46.

8. Symptoms of chronic overload—E.M. Gherman, *Stress and the Bottom Line: A Guide to Personal Well-Being and Corporate Health,* AMACOM, New York, 1981, p. 47.

9. 55% of U.S. workforce employed in information services—Karen Wright, "The Road to the Global Village," *Scientific American* (March 1990), p. 84.

10. Workload vs. time to do it—Julia Lawlor, "Messy Desk: What It Says About You," *USA Today* (June 18, 1991), p. A1.

11. More people make computers than cars—"The New Economy: Where the Action Really Is," *Globe and Mail* (August 25, 1992), p. B20.

12. Information-related tasks—Thomas Buckholtz, *Information Proficiency: Your Key to the Information Age,* Van Nostrand Reinhold, New York, 1995, p. 39 (From the Personnel Research and Development Centre, 1994 Report on the Survey of the Information Proficiency of Federal Employees [draft]).

13. Peter Drucker, *The New Realities,* Harper & Row, New York, 1989, p. 209.

14. Alvin Toffler, *Powershift,* Bantam Books, New York, 1990, pp. 168-169.

15. Al Ries and Jack Trout, *Horse Sense,* Penguin, New York, 1991.

16. The information gap—Alan Farnham, "The Trust Gap," *Fortune* (December 4, 1989), p. 58.

17. Study found employees don't believe managers—Bob Filipczak, "Obfuscation Resounding: Corporate Communication in America," *Training* (July 1995), p. 30.

18. The whole truth—Albert Karr, "Labor Letter," *Wall Street Journal* (February 4, 1992), p. A1.

19. What's that you say?—John Fielden and Ronald Dulek, "How to Use Bottom-line Writing in Corporate Communications,"

Business Horizons, Indiana University Graduate School of Business (July/August 1984), p. 25.

20. Malcolm Forbes, "Fact and Comment," *Forbes* (May 29, 1989), p. 19.

21. Top five issues for business communicators—Dennis Corrigan, "The Number One Issue for Professional Communicators," *IABC Communication World* (September 1992), p. 15.

CHAPTER 3: STAY CALM

1. Human mind can process seven factors—George Miller, "The Magical Number Seven, Plus or Minus Two: Some Limits on Our Capacity for Processing Information," *Psychology Review* (March 1956), pp. 81-97.

2. Peter McGugan, *Beating Burnout: Survival Guide for the 90's,* Potentials Press, Austin, Texas, 1989, p. 38.

3. Invention of the telegraph—"Information Age: People, Information and Technology." Permanent exhibit at the National Museum of American History, Smithsonian Institute, Washington, D.C.

4. President of real estate company has big information load—David Devoss, "If You Think You're Overloaded: 10 Southern Californians and Their Information Age Strategies," *Los Angeles Times Magazine* (January 22, 1989).

5. Electronic door—M. Salter, "Plug and Pray," *Globe and Mail* (Report on Business Magazine) (March 1995), pp. 94-95.

CHAPTER 5: DEVELOP INFORMATION-RECEIVING SKILLS

1. Careful and critical readers—John DiGaetani, Jane Boisseau DiGaetani, and Earl Harbert, *Writing Out Loud: A Self-Help Guide to Clear Business Writing,* Dow Jones-Irwin, Burr Ridge, Illinois, 1983, pp. 11-12.

2. Facts about files—"How to File and Find It," *Quill Business Library,* Quill Corp., Lincolnshire, Illinois, 1989.

3. Information guides—Thomas Davenport,

"Saving IT's Soul: Human-Centered Information Management," *Harvard Business Review* (March/April 1994), p. 130.

4. Satisfice—W. Russell Neuman, *The Future of the Mass Audience,* Cambridge University Press, New York, 1991, p. 96.

5. Reading trends—Ina Mullis and Lynn Jenkins, *The Reading Report Card 1971-1988: Trends From the Nation's Report Card,* Educational Testing Service, Princeton, New Jersey, 1990.

6. TV set on for 7 hours—*Nielson Media Research News,* A.C. Nielsen Company, 1990.

7. Where managers get information—Sharon McKinnon and William Bruns, *The Information Mosaic,* Harvard Business School Press, Boston, Massachusetts, 1992, pp. 162-164.

8. Dokikai—Alvin Toffler, *Powershift,* Bantam Books, New York, 1990, pp. 168-169.

CHAPTER 6: DEVELOP INFORMATION-SENDING SKILLS

1. Business writing principles—Tony Alessandra and Phil Hunsaker, *Communicating at Work,* Fireside, New York, 1993, p. 226.

2. C. Northcote Parkinson, *Parkinson: The Law,* Houghton Mifflin, Boston, Massachusetts, 1980, p. 203.

3. Guidelines to business audiences—John DiGaetani, Jane Boisseau DiGaetani, and Earl Harbert, *Writing Out Loud: A Self-Help Guide to Clear Business Writing,* Dow Jones-Irwin, Burr Ridge, Illinois, 1983, p. 23.

4. Political pros—John Doyle, "Blue Screen Effect," *Broadcast Week* (June 24-30, 1995), pp. 8-9.

5. You choose—Robert Haavind, "Hypertext: The Smart Tool for Information Overload," *Technology Review* (November/December, 1990), pp. 46-47.

6. Written and oral communication—Mary Finlay, *Communication at Work,* Holt, Rinehart and Winston of Canada Ltd., pp. 4-19.

7. Written and oral communication—Mary Finlay, *Communication at Work*, Holt, Rinehart and Winston of Canada Ltd., pp. 4-19.

8. Siegal & Gale—James Bredin, "Say It Simply," *Industry Week* (July 15, 1991), p. 20.

9. $2.79 mechanical pencil—Jeremy Main, "Battling Your Own Bureaucracy" in *Working Smarter* by the editors of *Fortune* magazine, Viking Press, New York, 1982, p. 81.

10. Typing speed vs. handwriting—Cheryl Currid, *Electronic Invasion: Brave New World of Business Communications*, Brady Computer Books, New York, 1993.

11. Why readers are good writers—John DiGaetani, Jane Boisseau DiGaetani, and Earl Harbert, *Writing Out Loud: A Self-Help Guide to Clear Business Writing*, Dow Jones-Irwin, Burr Ridge, Illinois, 1983, p. 7.

Index

About the Author

Maureen Malanchuk has more than a decade of experience as a communications professional in a variety of organizations and brings valuable "insider" knowledge about information networks and agendas to this book.

Most recently she worked for Bell Canada and Ontario's Ministry of the Attorney General, where she provided strategic communications advice on a number of major issues such as layoffs, reorganizations, and budget cuts. Maureen has also worked for an international oil company, an advertising agency, a professional association, and several not-for-profit organizations.

During her career, Maureen has edited a bi-weekly company publication distributed to 52,000 people and has written dozens of brochures, press releases, memos, information booklets, and speeches. Working in an information-intensive environment also has helped her to develop a number of coping strategies; during some of her major projects or when important issues would explode, it was not uncommon to find more than one hundred e-mail messages on her computer and her voice-mail system full.

Maureen's record of innovation and creativity is evident throughout her career as exemplified by her convincing a reluctant editor to switch to desktop publishing in the mid 1980s and then, several years later, developing one of the first programs of its kind in North America designed to facilitate communication between supervisors and their employees. She also initiated a program to provide employees with the information, tools, and skills they needed when the Canadian government opened up the long-distance market.

Maureen became increasingly interested in information overload while conducting numerous surveys and focus groups. The issue hit really close to home for her when audience members identified many of the information products she produced, such as newsletters and memos, in their lists of offenders. This finding forced her to look at her role as a contributor to other's information overload and inspired her to find a way to help audiences manage their flood.

Maureen has a B.A. in communications from Simon Fraser University in Vancouver, British Columbia. She and her husband now live in Vancouver. Maureen is currently developing a workshop and a software training program based on this book. She is also writing another book that examines the variety of strategies being tried by organizations, industries, and technologies to deal with the deluge.